Small-appliance Servicing

SMALL-APPLIANCE SERVICING

P. T. Brockwell, Jr.

McGraw-Hill Book Company, Inc.

New York   Toronto   London

1957

To Louisa

Preface

The purpose of this book is to acquaint its readers with professional small-appliance servicing techniques and ethical business procedures peculiar to such an enterprise. Some persons may regard the brief instruction in business methods as a secondary aim, but experience has proved that these two areas of training are so closely allied that one of them can hardly be considered without the other—particularly if the student wishes to prosper in this vocation.

Opportunities abound for the small-appliance repair specialist, for it is common knowledge throughout the industry that appliance-service business operators must almost invariably train their new service personnel to repair traffic appliances. Of course, in metropolitan areas a few men acquire small-appliance service experience by working in one of the factory repair centers, but in thousands of smaller communities a dealer may advertise for a traffic-appliance repairman for weeks and not get a single reply. So the field is wide open—and the training for this specialty can be had from this book in an incredibly short time.

Small-appliance Servicing is unique in its field in that its entire content is drawn from the author's 28 years' experience as an appliance-service specialist: a year and a half of which was spent in preliminary (on-the-job) training, seven and a half years as an appliance serviceman for a utility company, two years as a service manager for an appliance dealer, and seventeen years in his own service business.

No attempt has been made to cover all repair operations

on every small appliance, for such a thin spread of instruction would serve only to confuse the reader. Instead, the
seven appliances which the serviceman will most frequently
be called upon to repair are dealt with in realistic detail so
that he will be prepared to handle the problems which will
confront him *every* day. Thus grounded in the fundamentals, he will experience little or no difficulty in adapting
his basic knowledge to any of the other small appliances.
The advisability of such concentrated instruction has been
proved repeatedly in practice.

Because of its easy and gradual progression from the relatively simple operations to the more difficult, *Small-appliance Servicing* may be used effectively as an appliance-service primer in vocational schools. Its only prerequisite is
elementary electricity.

This book is equally well suited for self-instruction. Stu-
dents, as well as electrical workers in related skills who may
wish to expand their training to include small-appliance service, will appreciate the practical treatment of the subject.

Appliance dealers who now operate or plan to establish
their own service department may find *Small-appliance
Servicing* useful not only in guiding the business policy of
their service departments, but also as a training text for new
personnel to ensure uniform repair practices.

The author gratefully acknowledges the granting of the
book rights to him by the editors of *Electrical Merchandis-
ing,* in which magazine the bulk of this text and its illustra-
tions were first published in serial form under the title of
"Successful Small Appliance Service." The first two install-
ments appeared in the April and May, 1955, issues; the next
six, July to December, 1955, inclusive; and the ninth and
final installment was published in February, 1956.

P. T. Brockwell, Jr.

Contents

Introduction

Most of us like to watch an expert at work—even if his specialty differs from ours. Indeed, such an experience is often inspirational. For example, you might have happened upon an accident scene sometime where an electric-light pole had been broken off near its base, leaving the 30-foot shaft dangling from its wires like a pendulum. If you waited until the repairmen arrived, you must have been fascinated at how deftly they handled that ticklish task. Or possibly you have watched a wrecking crew clean up a railway collision and marveled at how perfectly every stage of that monstrous job was integrated. If you have witnessed a scene like one of these just described, you no doubt felt a sense of admiration for the experts who direct that sort of work. And to emulate such men in one's own specialty is praiseworthy, for too many mediocre mechanics are always at large.

In appliance-service work—as in any other skill—the service counselors, supervisors, and other leaders are chosen from that group of men who have attained an extra quality which puts them head and shoulders above the ordinary mechanics and classes them as experts. Furthermore, these are the men who are most likely to succeed in businesses of their own.

How do you feel about your future? Can you be satisfied with being just ordinary? Or do you envision yourself a few years from now as an expert, well qualified for a position of leadership? In either case, training and practice are two obvious essentials.

But if you wish to become an expert in the shortest possible time, there are two additional, equally important factors—habits, to be exact—which you must cultivate yourself. One of these is an inner urge to better your methods continually. This means undergoing a brief self-examination as you begin each new task by asking yourself this question: "How can I do this job better than I did the last?" Practice this idea until it becomes second nature, for it will not only lead you to make the best use of the general instruction contained herein, but also it will drive you to explore every source of specific information—all of which will speed your progress toward the realm of the experts.

Thoroughness is the other quality which you must cultivate in order to become an expert, for painstaking attention to every minute detail on every job is the only way to ensure safe and satisfactory operation of a repaired appliance. You cannot afford to skim over any part of the work, however trivial some items may appear.

In fact, a single act of negligence on the part of a repairman can result in serious personal injury to the appliance user. As one example, say that a serviceman has repaired a percolator by renewing the heating element, and in the course of the work found that the top handle-fastening screw was stripped, but he let it pass because the repair instructions mentioned only that the percolator would not heat. A little later that screw could work out while coffee is being poured, thereby allowing the pot to flip over and scald the user or some other member of that household. And though a serviceman can correct a faulty repair job by reworking it without charge, he can do nothing to ease the lifelong heartache of a disfigured human being.

Do not, however, conclude from the foregoing that an expert must sacrifice speed for thoroughness. On the contrary, actual speed in making repairs comes quickly to the careful worker because what he completes is well done—and though he may not seem to work as rapidly as those who go at their jobs helter-skelter, he rarely finds it necessary to do over any part of his work. Moreover, the most exacting final tests of a repaired appliance are not time-consuming at all—they are carried out with the aid of the testing apparatus while you are working on the next job. And although the preliminary tests to locate faults demand your undivided attention, most of these can be executed in seconds, for instead of connecting a heating appliance, for example, directly across the line and waiting to find out if it will heat, you energize it in series with a lamp whereby you can see immediately whether or not there is an unbroken circuit in the appliance. This preliminary series test, used with all small appliances, also eliminates the risk and subsequent delay of blowing the shop fuses in the event that the appliance under test is short-circuited.

Hence, using suitable equipment (which is described fully in Chap. 1) you can, after completing this study and with some practice, complete every small-appliance service job with reasonable dispatch and with full assurance that each is in safe and satisfactory operating condition.

CHAPTER 1

Testing Equipment

Not long ago the only testing device employed in most small-appliance service shops was a simple series tester consisting of merely a cleat receptacle, its lamp, the connecting cord, and a pair of testing points. And though adequate for yesterday's nonautomatic appliances, this scanty equipment alone on a repairman's bench today would be as out of place as a horse and buggy on an expressway.

1-1. Series Tester for Automatic Appliances. The series system is still used for the preliminary continuity test, even for automatic appliances, but you will note by referring to Fig. 1-1 (items 2, 3, 4, and 5) that the set illustrated includes also a 1,000-watt Edison-base heater coil which may be connected in parallel with the 25-watt lamp by closing the switch beside it. This adjunct enables you, by flipping a switch, to distinguish between a short circuit and an unbroken normal circuit in an appliance under test, either of which would cause the series lamp to light.

In operation, when you first connect an appliance (rated at approximately 75 watts or more) to the series test receptacle, the lamp will appear to glow to almost its normal brilliance if there is a closed circuit in the appliance. Then, to determine whether or not the appliance is short-circuited, you close the switch which connects the 1,000-watt tester

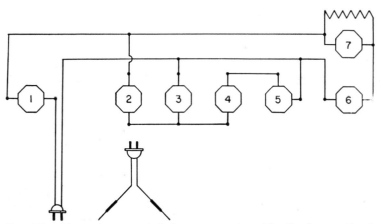

FIG. 1-1. The series tester and the power outlet with pilot lamp. Box 1 is for a 15-ampere fuse; 2, the series test receptacle; 3, the series test lamp; 4, the switch for the 1,000-watt tester coil; 5, the 1,000-watt tester coil; 6, the power outlet; 7, the miniature receptacle for the pilot lamp.

coil in parallel with the series lamp. If the lamp dims when you close the switch, no short circuit is indicated; but if the lamp continues to burn as brightly as before, the appliance is short-circuited.

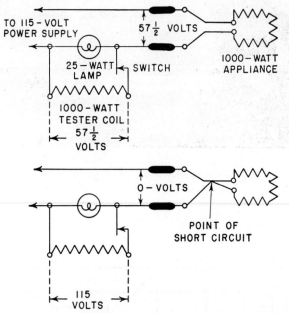

FIG. 1-2. Diagram of a 1,000-watt appliance connected to the series tester with the 1,000-watt tester-coil switch closed. The upper sketch shows the current flow through an appliance which is not short-circuited. The lower sketch illustrates the change which occurs when an appliance is short-circuited.

You will acquire facility in testing appliances with this equipment quickly if you understand why the tester responds in the manner just described. If, therefore, you wish to clarify the response by tracing the current flow, refer to Fig. 1-2. With a 1,000-watt appliance under test, as shown in the upper sketch, two low resistances are connected in series, between which the voltage is rather evenly divided because the wattages are approximately equal. Now it should be quite clear that the high-resistance lamp —which is tapped to one line terminal and at the midpoint between two nearly equal low resistances—will receive only about half its normal voltage and hence it will dim proportionately. But if the appliance element is short-circuited as shown in the lower sketch of Fig. 1-2, it also should be clear that full line voltage will flow unhindered directly to the parallel-connected lamp and the 1,000-watt tester coil.

1-2. Short-circuiting Loops. These are used frequently in conjunction with the series tester. For nearly every testing operation, two types of these loops will serve, one of which comprises a short length of flexible wire with an alligator clip attached to each end; and the other consists of several U-shaped pieces of solid copper or lead wire of assorted diameters so graded that each will fit snugly into the contacts of the terminal plug for which a particular loop is intended.

1-3. Test Cords. In addition to the test leads which have the prods on one end and an attachment plug on the other, testing-cord sets are employed not only in series testing, but also to connect across the line for a preliminary operating test an appliance whose cord set is not usable. These assemblies should be equipped with a variety of connectors (female plugs) and tips which will afford quick and easy temporary attachment to whatever types of appliances you service. To make up an initial assortment for general use, however, seven types of terminals usually will suffice; they are: (1) the standard heater plug, as used on most detachable iron cords, (2) the small heater plug, commonly used on many coffee-making appliance cords, (3) the roaster plug, which is somewhat larger than the standard iron plug, (4) straight wire tips (tinned), (5) eyelets, (6) compression sleeves, which are nothing more than the contacts from a standard heater plug, and (7) alligator clips. It goes without saying that the other end of each cord is to be fitted with a standard attachment plug.

1-4. Power Outlet with Pilot Lamp. When conducting an operating test on many of the automatic small appliances, you must be able to tell when the power is turned on

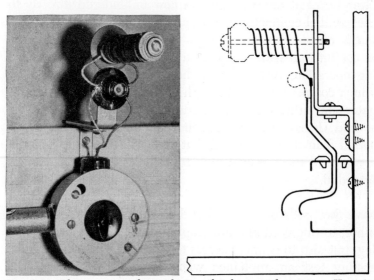

FIG. 1-3. The power outlet with its pilot lamp and resistor. Here is shown how the pilot lamp socket and its resistor may be fastened to the workbench backboard with common iron angle brackets.

and shut off automatically. Hence, this device is so designed that its lamp will glow only when current is being drawn from the outlet by an appliance rated at approximately 400 watts or more. See Fig. 1-3.

1-5. The Temperature Meter. This with its appurtenances (Fig. 1-4) will enable you to eliminate all guesswork in testing most of the automatic appliances in which accurate temperatures are essential to satisfactory operation.

1-6. Ground Indicator. Keep in mind that a grounded appliance often will operate satisfactorily in every other respect; hence, such a fault presents a hidden hazard, for the user is not aware of trouble until she has suffered an electric shock. Can a 115-volt shock be fatal? Yes. It depends, of course, upon the constitution of the individual as well as the material circumstances at the time of the accident. For this reason, it is obligatory that you run a continuous ground test while proving the work in order to make sure that no grounds occur in the appliance during *any* stage of operation. The ground indicator is a timesaver, too, in that an iron may be continuously ground tested throughout all other stages of checking while it is on the stand—without using the prods. This same type of ground test

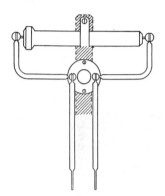

FIG. 1-3A. Alternate type of pilot lamp resistor, using 4 inches of No. 16 Nichrome wire. Fasten the insulating tube crosswise to the bracket with a strap, as shown, and use No. 16 solid stove wire for the leads.

may be applied to other appliances by clipping the extra ground-detector lead to some unpainted metal part of the outer shell of the appliance. See Fig. 1-4.

1-7. Hot-water Thermometer. An immersion-type mercury thermometer, especially designed for use in hot water, is used for testing the temperature of the water in a coffee-making appliance when you have reason to check the accuracy of its thermostat setting.

1-8. Tachometer. This enables you to check the spindle speed of a food mixer so that you will recognize the need for an adjustment of its governor mechanism.

1-9. How to Assemble the Series Tester and Power Outlet. In Fig. 1-1 is illustrated one of the cheapest and quick-

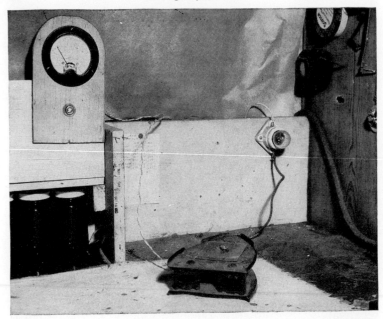

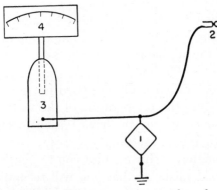

Fig. 1-4. Temperature meter, iron testing stand, and ground detector. Part 1 is an Edison-base cleat receptacle; 2, an extra lead and clip; 3, the testing stand; and 4, the meter.

est ways to build this equipment with standard electrical supplies. Use 3¼-inch octagon boxes and join them with ½-inch nipples, then fasten this assembly to the workbench backboard. Be sure to use insulating bushings where the cord set leaves box #1 and where the pilot lamp wires enter the power-outlet box. Connect the various devices as shown in the wiring diagram (Fig. 1-1), using No. 14 RC or similar wire between boxes and No. 14-2 heater cord with a polarized plug for the cord set.

One method of supporting the miniature cleat receptacle and its resistor is with common iron angle brackets (Fig. 1-3). The resistor is shown at the top; the miniature receptacle directly beneath. To make this resistor, wind about 11 feet of No. 18 bell wire on a 3-inch porcelain tube, leaving the leads long enough to reach into the outlet box below. Do not cut the wires at the miniature receptacle, but form an eye in each lead for tapping the respective terminals of the miniature receptacle. Use a one-cell flashlight bulb for this pilot lamp.

The resistor just described hums slightly when current (7 amperes or more) is passing through it. If you prefer to sacrifice this warning sound for less bulk, a mere *4 inches* of No. 16 Nichrome resistance wire may be substituted for bell wire. If you do use the Nichrome wire, connect the leads as shown in Fig. 1-3*A*.

1-10. How to Connect the Iron Testing Stand, Temperature Meter, and Ground Detector. Referring to Fig. 1-4, an Edison-base cleat receptacle (#1) for the ground-detector lamp is shown fastened directly to the workbench backboard. One terminal of this receptacle is wired to a good ground connection, the other is grounded to the iron testing stand (#3). An extra lead and clip (#2) is also to be connected to the same terminal of the receptacle as the iron testing stand. Use No. 18 stranded (fixture) wire for these connections. A 2-watt neon lamp in the ground-detector socket will provide a critical ground test, but this type of lamp is so sensitive to minute current leaks that you may get a dim reading from any appliance—good or bad—on a rainy day. For general use, an ordinary 7½-watt incandescent lamp will serve the purpose.

The iron testing stand (#3) is connected to the temperature meter (#4) with a special cable which must be purchased with the instrument. It is important to remember, however, that the wires in this cable must never be trimmed, because changing the length of the wires will impair the accuracy of the meter. Therefore, keep a spare cable on hand for immediate replacement when necessary.

Unit-type electric-iron testers are available in which the meter and stand are built into one assembly, but with the arrangement shown in Fig. 1-4 (separate meter and stand) you can use an oven-testing cable with the same meter for checking roaster temperatures. If you do use the one meter for both, it is a good idea to mount the meter, as illustrated, on a separate piece of plywood which should be fastened to the test panel with a single thumb screw. This method of support will give you easy access to the back of the meter where the terminals are located for changing the cable when you have to test a roaster. On the other hand, if you service many roasters, it may be more economical in the long run to purchase a separate thermocouple-type oven tester so that you can leave the iron testing stand permanently connected to the panel meter.

QUESTIONS

1. Why should an inoperative appliance be series tested before it is connected across the line?

2. With the series tester described in this chapter, how

would you distinguish between a short circuit and an unbroken normal circuit in an appliance under test?

3. Explain why it is necessary to run a continuous ground check while an automatic appliance is undergoing an operating test.

4. If an appliance is grounded, does it necessarily follow that it will not operate?

5. Most customers as well as employers will make reasonable allowances for human error, but of all testing and/or assembly errors in appliance-service work the most serious is that of returning to the user a grounded appliance which has been declared satisfactorily repaired by the serviceman. Do you agree with this statement? Give the reason for your answer.

CHAPTER 2

Cord Sets

Since the cord set suffers more abuse than any other part of a small appliance and hence is one of the common causes of failure, any small-appliance testing procedure should begin with the cord set. With this thought in mind we have elaborated upon testing as well as servicing cord sets in this early chapter as a preliminary step to all other testing and servicing procedures which are to follow. Take time enough now, therefore, to familiarize yourself with these elementary processes so that you may center your attention on testing and servicing procedures for the appliances proper when you take up the next seven chapters.

TESTING

2-1. A Detachable Cord Set. This is relatively simple to test because it may be disconnected and handled as a separate unit by merely withdrawing its connecting plug from the terminals of the appliance. For a thorough test follow the four steps listed below, but keep in mind that, in view of the nominal cost of a completely assembled new cord set, you would not in actual practice continue the test beyond any stage that proves the assembly to be unworthy of repair.

1. Visual examination. Inspect the cord itself for possible damage to its outer sheath and, if it appears to be sound in this respect, make sure that no broken ends of wire strands penetrate the outer covering. Now examine the attachment plug as well as the contacts in the connecting plug

FIG. 2-1. Testing for possible short circuits by pushing in the cord and twisting it slightly where it enters one of the plugs while the cord is connected in series with a 25-watt lamp.

for evidence of burning, for all these points of contact must be clean and bright and each must grip its mate tightly in order to ensure good electrical connections. If the cord set passes this inspection, continue as follows:

2. Short-circuit test. With the 1,000-watt tester-coil switch open, connect the cord set to the series test receptacle, push the cord in, and twist it slightly where it enters the plugs. See Fig. 2-1. The series lamp should stay out during this test, of course; but if in either of the plugs there are wires bared too far back from the point of connection,

this push-in-and-twist maneuver will unite them momentarily and cause the test lamp to flicker, thereby indicating a short circuit. If the response is favorable, go on to the next step.

3. Continuity test. With the cord set still connected to the series tester and the 1,000-watt tester-coil switch open, insert a snug-fitting, short-circuiting loop into the contacts

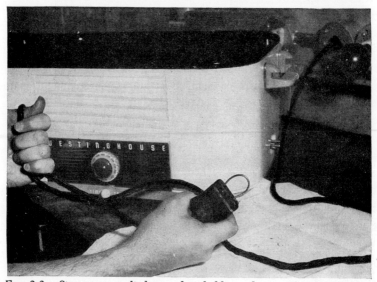

Fig. 2-2. Stress test applied to a detachable cord set. The short-circuiting loop can be seen protruding from the terminal plug.

of the connecting plug to close the circuit at that end of the cord. See Fig. 2-2. If the test lamp lights, stress-test the cord and its connections in this manner: Hold the attachment plug in the series test receptacle with one hand and, with the other, grasp the cord about 18 inches back from that end and jerk it moderately as though you were trying to snatch the cord from the plug; then continue this test by jerking short sections of the cord throughout its length as though you were trying to find a weak point where you might pull it apart. (This operation is also illustrated in Fig. 2-2.) Obviously, if there is a loose connection in one of the plugs or a broken conductor in the cord whose fracture is butt-ended, this treatment will cause the test lamp to flicker or to go out entirely. If the test lamp does not light, you may try a compression test (exact opposite of a stress test) in an effort to unite momentarily the disconnected parts and thus isolate the fault to one place or another. If the response is favorable, continue.

4. Load test. Leave the short-circuiting loop in the connecting plug with the other end of the cord set attached to the series test receptable as in testing step 3. Now if you question the cord's current-carrying capacity for reason of its age, or because you have noted a weak point where it seems to bend too easily as though all but a few strands of wire in either conductor are broken, you can readily impose a severe load test on the cord by closing the 1,000-watt tester-coil switch for a minute or two. Do not, however, risk injuring your hands by handling the cord while it is so connected, for one of its conductors may burn in two at a weak point. Rather, after you have subjected the cord to this load test, disconnect it before you check it for hot spots. In most instances the entire cord will get warm, but weak places will get extremely hot or burn in two.

2-2. A Built-in Cord Set. This is tested in a somewhat different manner from the detachable type because in most built-ins we do not have the same easy access to the connecting terminals. Remember, however, that in testing you seek to learn as much as possible about the cause of failure with little or no dismantling. To this end you should not remove a single screw unless it is necessary to complete a required stage of the test. Use the following four-step procedure for testing built-in cord sets, but—as explained in

Art. 2-1—you would in practice abandon the test at any stage that proves the cord set to be unworthy of repair.

1. Visual examination. Inspect the attachment plug, the cord, its outer sheath, and the cord guard (or spring and bushing) for exterior damage and make sure that no broken ends of wire strands have punctured the cord's outer sheath. If the cord set appears to be sound, continue as follows:

2. Short-circuit test. With the 1,000-watt tester-coil switch open, connect the appliance cord set to the series test receptacle and turn off the switch or the control on the appliance to ensure an open circuit in the cord. If the test lamp goes out when you turn off the appliance switch, give the cord the push-in-and-twist treatment as suggested in *Testing*, step 2, Art 2-1. The test lamp should stay out of course; if it does, go on to the next step. If for any reason you cannot turn off the appliance, or when you do, if the lamp continues to glow, you may still check for a short circuit by closing the 1,000-watt tester-coil switch; if the lamp dims, try the push-in-and-twist maneuver; if the lamp stays dim, you have ruled out a short circuit and you may continue with the next step. Usually the preceding tests will enable you to determine whether or not a built-in cord set is short-circuited. If, however, the lamp does not dim when you close the 1,000-watt tester-coil switch, your test has disclosed a short circuit, but it does not necessarily follow that the cord is at fault—it could be the appliance. For a final attempt to conclude this step without opening the terminal enclosure, leave the 1,000-watt tester-coil switch closed and try a gentle push-pull-and-twist treatment on the cord where it enters the plug and the terminal enclosure in an effort to separate momentarily bare wires which might have short-circuited at these points. If the appliance proper is not short-circuited, and you are able to separate any short-circuited conductors in the cord in this manner, the test lamp

will dim each time you separate the exposed wires. If this effort fails to isolate the fault, you must now open the terminal enclosure in order to disconnect one wire of the cord set, whereupon you should follow the same procedure for a short-circuit test as that suggested for detachable cords in *Testing*, step 2, Art. 2-1. If the response to this test is favorable, continue.

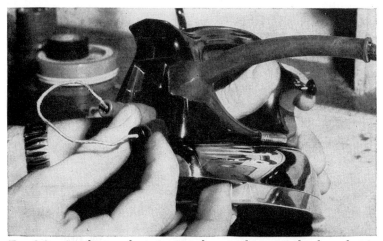

Fig. 2-3. Attaching a short-circuiting loop to the terminals of an electric iron.

3. Continuity test. With the 1,000-watt tester-coil switch open and the cord set still connected to the series test receptacle, close the circuit at the other end of the cord by turning on the appliance switch. If the appliance has a variable control, set it at the highest point; if it is an automatic toaster, depress the starting lever. But if you have had to open the terminal enclosure in the preceding step, leave it open and short circuit that end of the cord. Now if the test lamp lights, stress-test the cord as explained in *Testing*, step 3, Art. 2-1. If the lamp does not light, or if it flickers, try a compression test on the cord (also described in

Testing, step 3, Art. 2-1) in an attempt to bring together momentarily the ends of a broken conductor. If this effort fails to isolate the open circuit to the cord and you have not found it necessary up to this point to open the terminal enclosure, you must do so now so that you can clip a short-circuiting loop onto the terminals in order to complete the continuity test. See Fig. 2-3. If the response is favorable, continue.

4. Load test. If in a preceding step you have had to short circuit the cord in the terminal enclosure, you may load test the cord by the same method as that suggested for detachable cord sets in *Testing*, step 4, Art. 2-1. Otherwise, the load test should be deferred until series tests on the appliance itself have revealed that it is ready for a preliminary operating test during which the cord may then be checked for hot spots.

SERVICING

From the standpoint of good workmanship and economy, and to ensure long, uninterrupted service from a repaired appliance, renewal of the cord set is always preferred to repairing—except possibly for the replacement of the attachment plug or some such minor service. But inasmuch as you will be called upon to disconnect and reconnect many cord sets in the course of your work, this text would hardly be complete without instructions for the professional handling of this vital subassembly. And you must not conclude that, because many householders repair and install their own appliance cords, cord servicing is something anyone can do and is for that reason a subject to be passed over lightly. Many householders do repair their own—some have with disastrous consequences. Suffice it to say, therefore, that an amateurish cord repair or installation can render an appliance just as inoperative—and just as deadly— as any other incompetent servicing.

2-3. Initial Preparation. In preparing the ends of a length of appliance cord for connection, be sure to push one end of the unstripped cord through the attachment plug and the other end through the rubber sleeve, the spring, the bushing, or any other protective device and/or aperture in the appliance through which the cord must pass. Otherwise, it may be extremely difficult to force the prepared end of the cord through such openings.

2-4. Strain Relief. When connecting a cord set, you must provide strain relief at both ends to protect the electrical connections from mechanical stress. This protection is usually accomplished by snubbing the wires in a standard attachment plug as well as in heater plugs, and by the use of some form of clamp in terminal enclosures. The important point to remember is that the cord must be made mechanically secure ahead of the electrical connections.

2-5. Unsheathing Rubber Cord. The outer sheath of reinforced rubber cord is easily removed with a knife, but you must guard against cutting into the insulation of the individual conductors. After deciding how much of the sheath you need to remove, make a shallow diagonal cut *that* distance from the end of the cord and peel this narrow sliver off toward the end. Ordinarily, you will then be able to peel off the rest of the circumference of the outer sheath at the end of the cord, whereupon you can pull back the opened sheath as far as is necessary. Now trim the shaggy threads and the sheath and, if you do not need to use the jute or twine fillers for tying to a strain-relief device, cut these off flush with the sheath also. For extra neatness, you may seal the end of the cable where the wires emerge by binding with a few turns of friction tape not over a ¼ inch wide. (If you use the standard ¾-inch tape, split it.)

2-6. Stripping. If you use a knife instead of a wire stripper, be careful that you do not cut the fine wire strands as you strip the insulation from the individual conductors, for if you cut many you will reduce the current-carrying capacity of the cord. To be on the safe side, therefore, if you inadvertently sever more than one or two strands, trim the conductor off flush and begin again.

2-7. Unsheathing Heater Cord. The fabric outer sheath of heater cord is readily removed by unraveling with an awl. Begin unraveling at the end and work back a little at a time as far back as is required and trim the ragged ends of the outer braid with a pair of scissors. Now strip the tips of the individual conductors and attach eyelets if required, or, if straight wire tips are to be used, twist the strands tightly so that they will hold together well. If you are preparing the cord for connection in a heating-appliance terminal enclosure, bear in mind that because of the extreme heat at this point no friction tape should be used for insulation on this end of the cord. (While one manufacturer applies a small band of friction tape to the outer braid of the cord as padding under a metal strain-relief clamp, drying out of the tape in this instance, of course, can do no harm.) Instead of tape, asbestos string should be used to bind the fuzzy asbestos insulation of the separate conductors as well as the ragged ends of the outer braid of the cord.

Here is an easy method to follow which will enable you to lace the end of the cord neatly. After the outer braid has been cut back the required length and the tip ends of the wires have been properly stripped, form this prepared end of the cord into a Y. Begin with the asbestos string at the bottom of the Y by whipping down the ragged ends of the outer braid; then—using a coarse spiral overlay—bind the fuzzy asbestos insulation of one separate conductor almost to the end of the insulation. Make two or three turns at this end and return, making a similar overlay in the opposite direction to the bottom of the Y. Repeat the process on the second individual conductor finishing at the bottom of the Y where, after making a turn or two, you can tie the

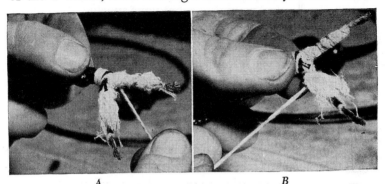

A   B

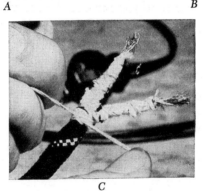

C

FIG. 2-4. Lacing the end of a heater cord. *A*, the serviceman has bound the braid where the conductors emerge and is starting to bind one conductor; *B*, he is about to bind the second conductor; and *C*, he has bound both and is shown tying the ends of the asbestos string at the starting point.

ends of the asbestos string together. When properly done, the individual asbestos insulated wires will be whipped with a crisscross effect. See Fig. 2-4.

2-8. Connecting. Every electrical connection must be tight. A loose connection not only impairs the efficiency of an appliance, but also is the forerunner of more serious trouble. Indeed, a loose connection in the terminal enclosure of an iron, for example, can develop enough excess heat to burn off a terminal in a short time. Make it a habit, therefore, to check all accessible connections when you service an appliance—no matter what your specific task happens to be.

In order to ensure that no "wild" strands of wire protrude from a connecting terminal, strip and trim each conductor to fit the connecting device precisely so that every strand is caught in the connecting clamp and the insulation butts right up to the binding screw, for one "wild" strand could cause a ground.

When untinned stranded wires are to be fastened directly under the head of a binding screw, make one complete right-hand turn of the conductor under the screwhead—no more, no less—and cross the free end of the wire over the starting point at a right angle. Less than one full turn would cause the strands to spread and the connection would soon loosen; more than a full turn would create a windlass effect and you would break more than half the strands before you could get the connection tight. It is a convenience, however, to strip a little more wire than is actually needed so that you can retain your hold on the free end of the wire as you tighten the screw. That is the quickest method of attachment with no risk of splaying the strands. After you have tightened the connection, nip off the surplus wire close to the binding screw with a diagonal plier.

Where a binding screw terminal is provided with special circular washers which are intended to hold the strands together, make one full turn of the wire, but in this type do not cross the free end over the starting point. Instead, form the bared tip of the wire into a U and then bring the free end as close to the starting point as is necessary to fit the cavity in the terminal washer.

Do not attempt to improve on a straight-tip pressure connection by making a circular turn of the wire under either the screwhead or the special washer. Rather, strip exactly the right length of wire to fill the channel in the terminal or its washer and tighten the screw securely. If the channeled washer or its terminal is distorted and will not grip the wire firmly, replace the necessary parts to ensure a tight connection.

2-9. Tinning. In attachment plugs, and in the terminal enclosures of appliances which accumulate little or no heat, you may tin the wires lightly as a means of holding the strands together, if you prefer this method, but you must not tin wires that are to be connected in a terminal enclosure where the temperature approaches the melting point of solder. Remember, too, that when forming the loop in a tinned wire under a binding screw you should not cross the free end over the starting point, for such an uneven doubling of tinned wire will not yield when you tighten the screw, with the result that you will not be able to compress the wire uniformly under the screwhead.

2-10. Splicing. Under no circumstances should an appliance cord be spliced. Splicing as referred to here concerns the connecting of the cord set to the interior wiring of an appliance. Virtually all such joints are made in one of two ways: (1) with insulated wire connectors, some of which will stand relatively high temperatures, or (2) with solder and tape, but only in enclosures where the heat rises little above room temperature.

In servicing small appliances you will not be called upon to make many soldered splices, but when you are, follow these four steps: (1) tin each conductor separately, (2) join them, (3) dab a little soldering paste on the splice, and (4) apply the heat. By this method you will fuse each wire to the other at every point of contact, thus assuring a strong joint with good electrical continuity. Finally, insulate the joint compactly but adequately so that its insulation is equal to that of the wires beyond the juncture.

When using any type of insulated wire connectors, measure accurately the length of wire to be stripped or trimmed so that no bare wire will be exposed outside the insulating thimble. And do not be discouraged if in your first few attempts to attach a screw-on wire connector you unintentionally wring off the wires, for a little practice will enable you to learn how to tighten this type of connector without mishap.

QUESTIONS

1. The testing procedures recommended herein for both detachable and built-in cord sets list four identically captioned steps. Name the four steps by their respective captions and in the order shown in the text.

2. What precaution should you take to avoid the possibility of personal injury when conducting a 1,000-watt load test on a cord set of dubious current-carrying capacity?

3. What should you do with a length of appliance cord immediately before you unsheathe it preparatory to connecting it to an appliance?

4. Why should no friction tape be used to insulate or to bind the wires which are to be connected inside the terminal enclosure of an iron?

5. Would you tin the stripped ends of wires as a means of holding the strands together which are to be connected in the terminal enclosure of an iron? Give the reason for your answer.

6. One or two "wild" strands of wire protruding from the terminals of an appliance could come together and thereby cause a short circuit, but a short circuit is by far the lesser

of two possible evils which could result from such careless connecting. What is the other?

7. If you had returned to a customer a repaired iron in good operating condition and the next day you found a strain-relief clamp on your workbench and only then realized that you unintentionally failed to replace this part, would you consider this an error serious enough to warrant your asking the customer to return the iron so that you could install the clamp? Give the reason for your answer.

8. Describe the method given in this chapter for lacing the individual insulated conductors of heater cord with asbestos string.

9. Explain how you would form and fasten untinned stranded wires directly under the head of a binding screw.

CHAPTER 3

Irons

There are two reasons why our discussion on servicing the appliances proper begins with irons: one is to enable you at the outset to become familiar with the operation of a bimetallic thermostat in one of its simplest forms, and the other is to afford you the opportunity to acquire facility in using the tester—without your being plagued with optional testing schemes for different models; for automatic iron circuits are so similar in design that you may follow a fixed testing procedure for almost any make or model.

COMPONENTS

3-1. Conventional Irons. Electrical components comprise a Nichrome heating element, a thermostat, the terminals, the terminal insulator, a cord set, and, in some makes, a pilot lamp and its resistor.

Mechanical parts include the soleplate, the pressure plate, the cover, the heel rest or other type of stand, the handle, and the strain relief for securing the cord set in the terminal enclosure. The first—and in some makes the first two parts —may be combined with the heating element to form a unit. In still other makes the element may be cast into the soleplate, in which case the pressure plate is not used.

3-2. Steam Irons. Steam iron parts include, in addition to the foregoing, a steam chamber and its appurtenances.

3-3. Travel Irons. Most of these compact, featherweight models—which add little bulk to one's baggage—feature a thin soleplate and cover assembly, a folding handle, and a trim carrying case. In every other respect their components are similar to those of the conventional models.

OPERATING PRINCIPLES

Though the operating theory of an electric iron may be regarded as elementary, two of its subassemblies and the steam model warrant a brief explanation of their operating principles.

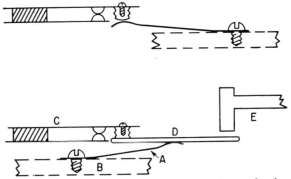

FIG. 3-1. An iron thermostat's basic parts. In the lower sketch, *A* is the bimetallic blade; *B*, the soleplate; *C*, the switch; *D*, the beam; and *E*, the control cam. The upper sketch shows a fixed thermostat.

3-4. Thermostat Operation. The most commonly used thermostat is relatively simple. See Fig. 3-1.

A bimetallic blade fastened at one end bends proportionately as the temperature of the soleplate rises and this motion is used to open the switch of the thermostat. As the temperature falls, the bimetallic blade begins its return toward its original position and the switch closes again. When the control knob is turned toward a higher temperature, the distance which the bimetallic blade must travel to open the switch is increased; when turned toward a lower temperature, the distance is decreased. Of course, how this is accomplished may vary with different manufacturers but the principle is essentially the same.

There may be still in service a few models with a fixed thermostat, or some with no thermostat at all, but these are now rarely seen.

3-5. Pilot Lamp. Low-voltage pilot (shunt) lamps, which indicate when the iron is heating, are connected in parallel with a resistor, while the resistor is connected in series with the heating element.

3-6. Steam-iron Operation. When the iron is hot and in steaming position, water from its reservoir flows to the steam chamber, which is either in or adjoining the soleplate. Here the water is vaporized and the steam is emitted through ports in the underside of the soleplate. Although a large number of self-contained makes and models have been produced, several have appeared with the reservoir outside the iron, and at least one manufacturer has produced a steam-ironing attachment which can be readily clamped to the soleplate of a conventional iron of the same make. Despite these differences in design, however, the operating principle is virtually the same.

TESTING

3-7. A Five-step Testing Procedure. Using equipment described in Chap. 1, place the iron on the testing stand and leave it there for every test in which the iron is connected through a cord set to the series tester or to a power outlet. If you must test the interior parts with the prods, though, remove the iron from the stand for that part of the operation only. Proceed in this manner:

1. Test the cord set as instructed in Chap. 2, employing whichever testing procedure (Art. 2-1 or 2-2) is appropriate for the type of cord set in hand. If the cord set is faulty, attach a test cord and continue.

Fig. 3-2. Beginning the series test.

2. Assuming that the iron now has a good cord set, either its own or a test cord, open the 1,000-watt tester-coil switch, connect the iron to the series test receptacle, and turn the control knob on the iron to its highest temperature. See Fig. 3-2. If the lamp does not light, an open circuit is indicated in the iron and you must test the element and thermostat separately with the prods. If the series lamp does light, continue as follows:

3. Close the 1,000-watt tester-coil switch. If the lamp does not dim to about half its normal brilliance, a short cir

cuit is indicated within the iron and the element and thermostat must be tested separately.   If the lamp does go dim, proceed as follows:

4. Revolve the control knob from one extreme to the other, observing whether or not the test lamp stays half-

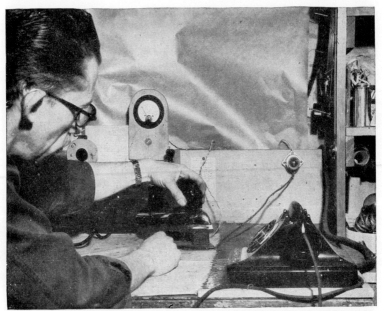

FIG. 3-3.   Revolve the control knob from one extreme to the other with the 1,000-watt tester-coil switch closed.   The series lamp should stay half-bright through all the *on* stages and go out at the *off* point.   The ground-indicating lamp should not light during any testing stage.

bright through all the *on* stages, and that it goes off at the *off* point.   See Fig. 3-3.   Transpose the polarity of the circuit by reversing the attachment plug in the series test receptacle and again revolve the control knob from one extreme to the other.   All during this step, watch the ground-indicating lamp on the tester to be certain that it stays *out*. If it does light, a ground is indicated and the fault must be located and corrected before proceeding further.

5. The iron is now ready for the final test, provided the preceding tests have established that there is a closed circuit

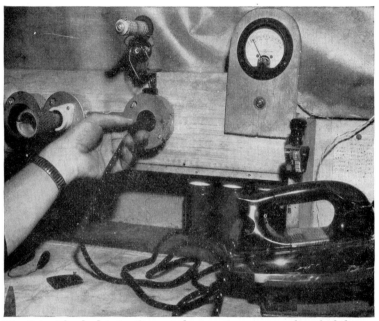

Fig. 3-4. The final test. Connect the iron to a power outlet which has a pilot lamp so that you can check the shut-off and turn-on temperatures.

in the iron; but no short circuits, loose connections, nor grounds. With equipment described in Chap. 1, this test will disclose not only whether the temperature is correct through several settings of the thermostat, but also it will indicate any intermittent grounds. It must be remembered that such grounds can occur as the temperature rises, which would not show when the iron was tested cold, for the thermostat parts move as the iron heats and any misalignment or distortion of these parts could result in a ground at a higher temperature. Bear in mind that *a grounded appliance subjects the user to a serious accident hazard* and for this reason no effort should be spared to make certain that no grounds exist at any temperature.

Disconnect the iron from the series test receptacle and connect it to the power outlet which has been equipped with a pilot lamp. See Fig. 3-4. Set the control knob at *Rayon* and allow the iron to heat while you are beginning the next job. Meanwhile, glance occasionally toward the pilot lamp and the temperature meter to guard against excessive overheating, using the temperature chart shown on page 35 as a guide. (If a tolerance chart for the make under test is at hand, use that instead.) Also remember that the ground-indicating lamp should not light throughout this test.

Since this final test is to determine whether the iron shuts off and comes on automatically at several points on the scale, do not move the control knob to the next higher stage until the iron has shut off and come on automatically at least once. This point cannot be overemphasized, for it should be made quite clear that if you even touch the control knob while the thermostat is automatically off, you help the thermostat complete a part of its function. In other words, you not only want to know that the power is turned off within the limits of a particular setting, but also that it is restored within those limits.

Now if the test so far has revealed that the iron maintains a temperature suitable for rayon, move the control knob up to *Wool* and check this stage. Finally, advance the knob to *Linen*. If these three stages are reasonably accurate, you may assume that the intermediate points are in proportion.

The following tolerance chart will serve for general use and whenever the chart for a specific make is not available.

Temperature Tolerances

Rayon	175–225°
Silk	225–350°
Wool	325–450°
Cotton	425–550°
Linen	525–600°

REPAIRING

3-8. Preparation. In order to protect the finish of the iron while you are repairing it, clear a space of any loose parts and tools about 18 inches square near the front center of your workbench and pad that area with several thicknesses of soft cloth. Then beyond this padded section (toward the back of the bench), place a small tray to receive the parts as you remove them from the iron. Finally, lay out the tools most likely to be used for the job in hand on one side or the other of the padded area, put your job orders and time records on the side of the bench opposite your tools, and you are off to a good start.

3-9. Disassembling. Though the method of disassembling a conventional iron varies with different makes and models, two or three methods are common to several. For example, on a number of makes you would follow this sequence: remove the terminal-enclosure cap, disconnect the cord set, remove the control knob, take out the cover screws, and lift off the cover and handle assembly as a unit. On certain models of two other makes, you would remove the heel cover plate to expose four screwheads, loosen the two inside screws but remove the two outside screws in the heel cavity, and slide the handle toward the back of the iron to remove the handle and the cord set as a unit, thereby allowing access to the cover screws. On still another make, you would remove the terminal-enclosure cap, disconnect the cord set, and then remove the escutcheon from the handle base to gain access to the cover screws. A careful examination of the iron will usually reveal the logical method of disassembly.

When you must pry off an escutcheon or a control lever situated over a chromium-plated, or other type of, finished surface, slip a piece of soft cardboard between the surface and the shank of the tool to avoid damaging the finish. And

Fig. 3-5. Two types of iron thermostats. One is adjustable, the other is not. The regulating screw is plainly visible in the rectangular type.

it matters not what type of wrench you use—socket, box, or open end—on nuts or cap screws which are tightened against a finished surface, slide a cardboard washer over the screwhead or nut so that the jaw or the face of the wrench as you turn it will not scar the finish.

3-10. Heating Elements. Heating elements should be renewed if they are open, grounded, or otherwise faulty. No patching should be attempted.

3-11. Thermostat Adjustment. Thermostats may be adjusted up or down the entire scale if they are provided with a regulating device. See Fig. 3-5. For example, if a thermostat is sound in every other respect and the heat test reveals that the temperature is, say, 120 degrees too high in every stage tested, it follows that an adjustment is advisable. Under no circumstances, however, attempt to adjust a thermostat which has no provision for adjustment—renew it.

Moreover, any type of thermostat must be replaced if it operates erratically, if grounded, if its switch points are inclined to stick, or if it is faulty in any other particular. Keep in mind that an iron with a short-circuited thermostat can accumulate enough heat to melt an aluminum soleplate.

3-12. Replacing Thermostats or Elements. When replacing these internal parts, do not fail to provide safe clearance between the current-carrying parts, and between these and other metal parts to ensure against short circuits and grounds. Test for short circuits and grounds before and after installing the cover.

3-13. Control Knobs. These are positioned by setting the control shaft to the *off* extreme—which is easily ascertained with the series test lamp—and then installing the knob so that it points precisely to the *off* marking.

3-14. Cord Sets. As pointed out in Chap. 2, except for replacing the attachment plug, more labor is expended in repairing a cord set than in renewing it. Furthermore, even more labor is saved if genuine cord sets are used in preference to either the fit-all variety or those assembled from bulk supplies in the shop.

3-15. Genuine Cord Sets. Those supplied by each manufacturer for his own make and model are fitted with the proper eyelets or other terminals, together with the strain relief and/or cord guard if required. And although these assemblies may cost somewhat more than any make-do cord set, the labor saved offsets the difference and the finished job presents a more professional appearance.

3-16. Replacement Cord Sets. Whether fit-all or assembled in the shop, these should equal in current-carrying capacity and in every other quality the cord set originally supplied with the iron.

3-17. Terminals and Terminal Insulator. In nearly every make iron, some type of insulating bushing is used where the terminals pass through the cover. Not only must you be sure that the terminals are clean and bright to ensure a good electrical connection, but also see to it that the insulator is intact and that the terminals are precisely centered in the cover opening so that the insulator will not be cracked when you tighten the cover.

3-18. Mechanical Work. Careful observation and good judgment on your part will enable you to do neat and workmanlike mechanical repairs. Handles, control knobs, terminal box covers, and all other miscellaneous parts should be replaced in the same manner in which they were originally installed by the manufacturer. Every part, however insignificant any may seem, has its place and purpose. Neither add nor take away—and never improvise.

And although a slightly chipped control lever or a cracked terminal box cover may appear to have no effect on satisfactory operation, renew any such damaged parts so that the finished job will be completely whole.

3-19. How to Remove Tight or Damaged Screws. The best way to avoid difficulty with tight screws is to use the most suitable tool for the purpose. As an example, for slotted screws—which are more often a source of trouble—use the largest screwdriver that will fill the slot. Inside the iron, particularly, where the screws are subjected to rather high temperatures, there are three preliminary steps from which you may select one or more to aid you in removing a tight screw: (1) apply penetrating oil and allow it time enough to work its way in, (2) try tightening the screw before you attempt to loosen it, (3) if there is no risk of damaging other parts, strike the screw a sharp blow squarely on its head; if it is a slotted-type screw, hold a solid shank screwdriver in the slot and hit the screwdriver with your hammer. If you either break off half of the head of a fillister-head screw or damage its slot, you may be able to remove it with a small pipe wrench. Hexagonal and square-head screws seldom present a problem, for you can usually get good leverage on these with a box-type or socket wrench without damaging the head.

If you are confronted with the problem where you have broken off a screwhead and some of the shank is protruding from the soleplate, apply penetrating oil to the threads, allow it to soak a few minutes, then put the screw stump in the vise and turn the soleplate with your hands, first in one direction and then in the other. After several such alternating twists, you may be able to unscrew the stump.

When you have inadvertently wrung off a screw flush with the soleplate, your first thought no doubt would be to drill a pilot hole in the damaged screw and attempt to remove it with a screw extractor. In a number of makes such an attempt—which may fail—would be false economy, for the price of a new soleplate may be less than that of the required labor for this tedious operation. You should, therefore, compare the price of a new soleplate with that of the estimated labor before making a decision in this regard.

3-20. Steam Irons. Every student of small-appliance servicing should be given an opportunity to disassemble and reassemble at least one standard-make steam iron. As previously pointed out, however, steam models vary widely in design with different manufacturers and for that reason no general disassembling and reassembling instructions can be given here which would be common even to any two makes. But it is reasonable to assume that schools using this text will have available one or more steam irons (as well as other appliances) for laboratory use. This chapter, therefore, should be supplemented with the manufacturer's service manual sheet for whatever-make steam iron is used for study.

In actual practice, though, steam irons may be put to preliminary electrical tests, like those used for conventional models, to ascertain the cause of failure in this particular; and a "live" operating test will disclose any leaks or other malfunction of the steaming apparatus. Then if only exterior repairs are needed, there is no reason why this service cannot be handled in an independent repairman's or a dealer's shop. Beyond this proceed with extreme caution— there are two reasons:

1. Some manufacturers offer an exchange plan to customers whose steam irons require major repairs whereby the customer can get a new or factory-rebuilt steam iron (which cannot be told from a new one) for much less than the price of a new iron outright.

2. Specific training, special tools, and a rather complete stock of parts should be acquired before attempting major repairs on steam irons. Inasmuch as only a small proportion of the irons received for repairs are steam models, and out of this small number only a few require major service, it would seem hardly worthwhile for an independent repairman or a dealer to make the initial investment—at least until sufficient volume justifies this step.

In any case, therefore, find out from the nearest service station what type of service policy applies to a particular make and model.

This farming out of major steam-iron service does not impose a hardship on customers, for a steam iron is most often the second iron in a house.

3-21. Shortest Route to the Top. Before affixing your stamp of approval to any job—whatever the extent of the service—subject it to every test shown under *Testing* (Art.

3-7) and, if it is not perfect in every respect, make it so. Experience has proved that scrupulous attention to every detail is not only profitable, but also leads to a growing circle of grateful customers.

QUESTIONS

1. What ruinous damage to an iron could result from a short-circuited thermostat?

2. What other part or parts would be damaged if a pilot-lamp resistor (or shunt) burned in two?

3. If a pilot-lamp resistor burns in two, would this fault render the iron inoperative?

4. In the five-step testing procedure you were instructed to leave the iron on the testing stand for every testing stage in which the iron was to be tested through a cord set. Can you give the reason for this?

5. The final testing step (operating test) is intended to prove two points, one of which is that the iron maintains a suitable temperature on various settings of the control. What is the other fact that this final test should establish?

6. Would you attempt to adjust a thermostat which operates erratically?

7. Would you try to mend a thermostat whose switch points have stuck?

8. Some control knobs are indexed to the thermostat shaft by means of a key, or some similar method, so that it is impossible to position the knob incorrectly. Explain how you would install a splined-hub control knob—that is, one which may be fitted to the shaft in any one of several positions.

9. Name at least two preliminary steps you would take to facilitate the removal of an extremely tight machine screw.

10. If you had wrung off a stud bolt flush with the sole-plate of an iron and you had to decide whether (1) you

should drill a pilot hole in the screw and attempt to remove it with a screw extractor or (2) renew the soleplate, what would your decision be if the price of a new soleplate was about the same as that of a half-hour's labor?

11. With some appliances a serviceman might attempt certain repairs experimentally—that is, unguided by specific training or service literature. In contrast to the method whereby one acquires advance training and/or adequate service literature for a particular make and model, experimental servicing is by far the slower, but it has been used repeatedly by skilled repairmen with excellent results. Yet, for major steam-iron repairs such a pick-your-way practice would be sheer folly. Do you agree with this last statement? Give at least one reason for your answer.

CHAPTER 4

Toasters

Many servicemen, though thoroughly skilled in some similar field of appliance repairing, are baffled when called upon infrequently to service an automatic toaster. Lack of practice, of course, contributes to such frustration. But—whatever variety or volume you may be assigned in the course of your work—if you know what is inside an automatic toaster, what those parts are supposed to do, and how each carries out its purpose, you should be able to go from the initial continuity test to the repairs and thence to the operating check in a methodical manner with few, if any, false movements.

COMPONENTS

4-1. Electrical Parts. In every automatic toaster there are a group of heating elements, a cord set, a timer, one or more switches, and a color control by which the user may vary the time cycle. At least one make is equipped with an electric motor which is used for actuating the bread carriage.

The timer for some models is supplemented by a thermostatic compensator which further regulates the time cycle automatically in proportion to the accumulated heat in the toaster so that any number of slices of bread may be toasted

43

successively and uniformly brown regardless of the temperature of the toaster at the beginning of any cycle. Still other timers are so designed that they are self-compensating.

4-2. Mechanical Parts. The principal mechanical parts common to oven-type toasters include the bread carriage with its lowering, holding, and lifting mechanism, the guide wires which flank the toasting slots to prevent the bread from coming into direct contact with the heating elements, the frame, the outer shell, the base, and the crumb tray. On models which require it, a check is employed to retard the speed of the rising carriage.

And in addition to such ordinary controls as the starting lever and the color selector, on some models you will find a *Crisper* (or *Melba*) knob and on some others, a *Keeps Warm* control. Then in sharp contrast, you will note that the fully automatic models have only a color-selector button.

Keep in mind the basic parts which are common to most automatic toasters, but do not at this point attempt to memorize the various special-control features, for each is discussed in detail in the evolution of the toaster mechanism under *Operating Principles*. As you study that section and its simplified sketches, you will experience little or no difficulty associating a particular control feature with some specific type of mechanism.

OPERATING PRINCIPLES

Let us begin with some of the relatively simpler mechanisms and work up gradually to the more complex models.

4-3. Clock-timed. See Fig. 4-1. Almost everyone—in and out of the trade—is familiar with this early design of the automatic pop-up toaster which employed a spring-motored clock to time the toasting cycle. To start this type, the user —by pushing down the starting lever(s)—wound the clock, lowered the carriage and latched it, and closed the switch. At the end of the time cycle the clock tripped the carriage latch and the elevating spring lifted the carriage with the toasted bread. A color control (*light* to *dark*) enabled the user to vary the time cycle by altering the speed of the clock. To get uniform toast from both hot and cold starts without changing the color control on this model, it was necessary to preheat the toaster for the first slice of bread.

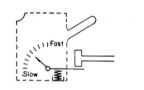

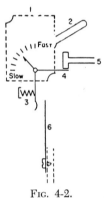

Fig. 4-1.   Fig. 4-2.

Fig. 4-1. A simple spring-motored clock timer.

Fig. 4-2. A spring-motored clock timer with thermostatic compensator. Part 1 is the clock assembly; 2, winder lever which is linked to the starting handle; 3, spring for the regulating arm; 4, the regulating arm; 5, the color control cam; and 6, the bimetallic blade.

Although thousands of these clock-timed toasters rendered excellent service over long periods of time—many having been in use for more than 20 years—the manufacturers of this type, prompted by the urge to make everything easier for the American housewife, modified this model by adding a thermostatic compensator.

4-4. Clock-timed with Compensator. (See Fig. 4-2.) The compensator comprises two parts: (1) a bimetallic blade which bends proportionately as the temperature increases inside the toaster, and (2) a spring-loaded regulating lever on the clock which is actuated by the bimetallic blade. (This regulating lever is independent of the color control and, of course, does not change its position.) As the toaster temperature rises, the bimetallic blade moves toward the clock-regulating lever, later striking it, and still later moving the lever to increase the speed of the clock. Thus the time cycle is varied automatically to suit the starting temperature of the toaster. The color control is the same as that used on the preceding model, but with this later design it is possible to get uniform toast whether started hot or cold without changing the color control or preheating.

4-5. Shock Absorber. Before moving-picture producers had too much fun depicting breakfast scenes in which an automatic toaster ejects the toast high into the air, most toaster manufacturers added a checking device—similar to a screen-door check—to retard the speed of the rising carriage as it neared the top of the slot.

4-6. Single-stage Thermostatically Timed. (See Fig. 4-3.) This method, in which the bimetallic blade is in direct contact with the bread, utilizes the principle that time is required for the blade to respond to heat. Conveniently, still more time is added to the toasting cycle if fresh, moist bread is used, for heat—as we all know—is carried away as moisture evaporates. On the other hand, if dry bread is used, heat accumulates more rapidly inside the toaster and the thermostat blade begins its movement toward the switch proportionately sooner. Thus, this type of timing adjusts itself automatically to accumulated heat and to almost any texture of bread.

Early applications of this principle included not only oven-type models, but also flip-over toasters. When one of these models shuts off at the end of the time cycle, a signal bell informs the user that it is time to flip the toast or

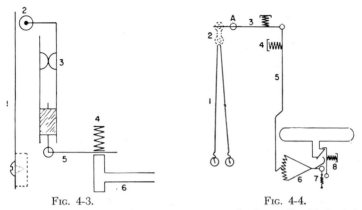

FIG. 4-3.   FIG. 4-4.

FIG. 4-3. A single-stage thermostatic timer. The bimetallic blade (1), which is in direct contact with the bread, curls toward the right as the temperature rises until the end of the time cycle when it strikes the switch insulator (2), opening the switch (3). The switch tilting arm (5) is held against the color control cam (6) by the spring (4).

FIG. 4-4. Hot-wire carriage-latch release. The hot wire (1) is shown at the left, fastened at the bottom to two terminals with its upper end passed through the insulator (2) on one end of the lever (3), whose fulcrum is at A. A spring keeps a downward pressure on the right-hand end of the lever (3). When the user depresses the carriage, it is held down by the spring-loaded latch (8). As the toaster heats, the hot wire (1), being in series with the elements, heats and expands, allowing the lever (3) to go down slightly on the right-hand end. This downward motion is transmitted to the pawl lever (5), which slips easily over the rachet-edge of the sector (6). A soft spring (4) holds the pawl gently against the sector. Now when the thermostat shuts off the hot wire cools and contracts, resulting in a slight upward motion on the right-hand end of the lever (3), which is transmitted through the pawl lever (5) to the sector (6), tripping the latch (8). As the carriage rises, it strikes the off-set in the pawl lever (5), disengaging it from the sector (6) so that the centering spring (7) may return the sector to its proper position for the next cycle.

to trip the carriage latch, as the case may be. The signal bell is actuated by a low resistance electromagnet.

The color control enables the user to vary the distance the bimetallic blade must travel to open the switch.

Further development of the preceding models includes the pop-up feature to replace the signal bell.

The hot-wire principle (see Fig. 4-4) is employed in this type to draw the carriage-latch release. A slender loop of special wire shaped like a hairpin with long legs has its upper portion—the loop—pulled tautly over the insulated end of a lever. The ends of the two legs are fastened to terminals which serve not only to anchor the ends of the hot wire, but also to connect it in series with the heating elements. Now when the user closes the main switch by depressing the carriage, the current flows through the hot wire thereby heating and expanding it. This small movement, which is transmitted to the lever at the point where the loop passes over, is multiplied at the other end of the lever by the position of the fulcrum. As the lever moves with this gradual expansion, it gathers a grip on the carriage-latch release. At the end of the time cycle the thermostat shuts off the current, the hot wire cools, contracts, and draws the carriage-latch release.

In addition to the color control, some of these models featured a *Crisper* or *Melba* selector. This device serves to interrupt the heating an increasing number of times during one cycle, depending upon how far the control is advanced toward *crisp*. These interruptions, of course, result in slower toasting and therefore crisper toast.

The *Crisper* comprises an adjustable escapement combined with the carriage-latch release. If this control is set at a point which would cause, for example, three interruptions, the thermostat would shut off the current thrice before the carriage pops up; for—while with each shutoff the hot wire will cool and contract—instead of tripping the carriage latch the first three times, it will draw three increments on the escapement. On the fourth thermostatic shutoff, however, the escapement is spent and locked so that the movement caused by the contraction of the hot wire is transmitted through the locked escapement to draw the carriage-latch release.

4-7. Single-stage Thermostatically Timed with Auxiliary Heater. This principle is similar to other single-stage thermostatic timing except that it employs a small auxiliary heating element, situated directly adjacent to a somewhat heavier thermostat blade than those used in other types of timers, which snaps with sufficient force to trip the carriage latch and open the switch. Earlier models of this design did not have the pop-up feature, but were automatic in every other particular. A pilot lamp informed the user when the toast was done, then the carriage had to be raised manually.

4-8. Automatic-carriage Movement. In this type the carriage descends almost magically after the bread is dropped into the slot and a minute or so later the finished toast rises quietly. No levers are necessary—the only control in sight is the color-selector button.

This is the operating principle of one make which uses single-stage thermostatic timing: The weight of a slice of bread when dropped into the slot depresses a lever which, through a linking mechanism, trips the switch to the *on* position where it remains until it is tripped *off* by the thermostat. With the current on, the hot wire expands allowing the carriage to descend. At the end of the time cycle the thermostat trips the switch to the *off* position, whereupon the hot wire cools and contracts, thereby lifting the carriage to its upper position. As the toast is lifted from the slot the starting lever in the carriage returns to its upper position and the toaster is prepared for the next cycle.

In another make, featuring the automatic-carriage movement, an electric motor is employed to pull down the carriage, but in this brand two-stage thermostatic timing is used.

4-9. Two-stage Thermostatically Timed with Auxiliary Heater.

(See Fig. 4-5.) This method is termed two-stage because the thermostatic timing cycle is in two parts: heating and cooling. A small auxiliary heating element is

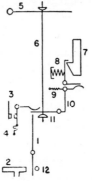

Fig. 4-5. Two-stage thermostatic timing with auxiliary heater. This sketch shows a part of the mechanism at the beginning of a cycle with the carriage (7) already latched down. The bimetallic blade (1) in this type of timer is pivoted as shown. As the auxiliary element heats the bimetallic blade, it bends on both sides of the pivot toward the left until the free movement of the lower part of the blade is hindered by the color-control cam (2); this causes the upper end of the blade to exert pressure against and to close the auxiliary switch (3), short-circuiting the auxiliary heater. (An overcenter spring is shown as part 4, which gives the auxiliary switch a snap action.) The bimetallic blade now begins its second stage of timing—cooling. It can be seen that before the blade had reached its left extreme, the trip link (11) dropped slightly and into the path of the returning bimetallic blade. As the blade nears the starting point, it will strike the link (11) moving the tripping arm (10) toward the right, thereby tripping the latch (8). Then the rising carriage, on reaching the top, will lift the reset lever (5) transmitting an upward motion to the trace (6), which in turn lifts the link (11) above the blade and reopens the auxiliary switch to prepare the mechanism for the next cycle. A centering spring for the tripping arm (10) is shown as 9; 12 is the cold-position regulating stop.

wrapped around the bimetallic blade and is connected in series with the main heating elements. There are two switches in this mechanism, a main switch and a short-circuiting switch for the auxiliary heater.

When the carriage is depressed, the main switch is closed,

but the short-circuiting switch for the auxiliary is open, which allows the auxiliary to heat along with the main elements. As the auxiliary heats, the bimetallic blade begins its movement toward a regulating stop. When the blade strikes the stop, the short-circuiting switch is closed, thereby bypassing the auxiliary heating element, although the main elements continue heating. The cooling bimetallic blade now begins its second stage of timing—its return toward the starting point. As the blade reaches the end of this return movement, it trips the carriage latch, the carriage rises, and the toaster is ready for another cycle.

4-10. Keeps-warm Control. This simple mechanical adjunct with a selector knob indicating *keeps warm* in one position and *pops up* in the other is incorporated into several makes. If this control is set at *keeps warm,* the current will shut off as usual at the end of the cycle, but the carriage will not rise until the user trips the latch.

4-11. Concentrate on Three Timers. Of the five more commonly used timing mechanisms just described, about 90 per cent of the toasters you will be called upon to service will be equipped with one of the following types of timers:

1. Clock with compensator
2. Single-stage thermostatic
3. Two-stage thermostatic with auxiliary heater

Obviously, if you become thoroughly familiar with these three basic principles of timing, it will be easy for you to grasp any slight variation in design.

TESTING

4-12. A Six-step Testing Procedure for Toasters. Prepare the series tester by opening the 1,000-watt tester-coil switch. Then, with the toaster right side up—and this is important, for in some makes the switch is held closed only by the weight of one of its members—and fully assembled, including the crumb tray, proceed in this manner:

1. Move the color control all the way to the *dark* extreme and try to get the toaster in the *on* position by lowering the carriage. If the model under test has an automatic-carriage

Fɪɢ. 4-6. To distinguish between a short circuit and an unbroken normal circuit when the test lamp lights, close the 1,000-watt tester-coil switch. The lamp should dim to about half its normal brilliance.

actuator, use the eraser-end of a pencil to depress once and immediately release the switch-tripping lever in the slot marked *one slice*. Connect the toaster to the series test receptacle and test the cord set as instructed in Chap. 2. If the cord set is faulty, attach a test cord and continue.

2. At this point the toaster should have a workable cord set. If the series lamp is now lighted, close the 1,000-watt

tester-coil switch. See Fig. 4-6. The lamp should dim to about half its normal brilliance; if it does, skip step 3. If it does not, a short circuit is indicated and it must be corrected before proceeding further. If the lamp does not light, continue as follows:

3. With the toaster still connected to the series tester,

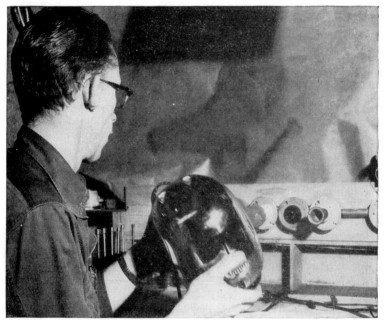

Fig. 4-7. Pressing the starting lever slightly below the latching point in an effort to close momentarily a faulty switch.

open the 1,000-watt tester-coil switch, and try pressing the carriage lever down a little deeper than the latching point, see Fig. 4-7, (this would not apply to an automatic-carriage actuator model); if this added pressure does not cause the lamp to flicker or to come on, take the toaster in both hands and shake it violently; first, from side to side, then up and down. If the switch is faulty, this maneuver may enable you to get it closed momentarily, at least long enough to do the ground test and to check the elements. If it does, continue with step 4; if it does not, enough of the mechanism will have to be exposed to test and/or examine the internal parts separately.

4. For the ground test, clip the lead wire from the ground-indicating lamp to some metal part of the toaster shell and

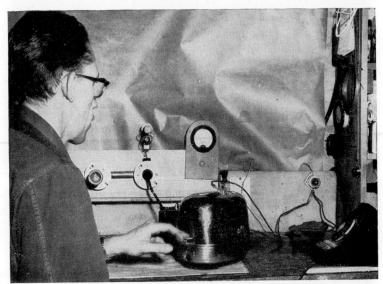

Fig. 4-8. The preliminary heating test. Note the extra lead from the ground detector clipped onto the top of the toaster's outer shell.

move the carriage up and down repeatedly. Now transpose the polarity of the circuit by reversing the attachment plug in the series test receptacle, and again move the carriage up and down. The ground-indicating lamp should stay out, of course, throughout this test. If the toaster is grounded, the fault must be corrected before continuing.

5. With the ground-indicating test lead still attached to the toaster body, disconnect the toaster's cord set from the

series receptacle and connect it to the power outlet which has a pilot lamp. See Fig. 4-8. Let the toaster heat just long enough to see whether all elements are heating, then

FIG. 4-9. The final test must be done with bread.

shut it off. Now allow the toaster to cool to room temperature while you are working on your next job, after which you can proceed with the final test.

6. There is but one way to do the final test—with bread which should be day-old and of uniform texture. See Fig. 4-9. Set the color control on *medium*, and toast several slices successively, occasionally allowing a moment to elapse

between toastings. (In practice, this is not a time-consuming test, for with the toaster at one end of the workbench you can work on another job.) The bread should toast rather uniformly from hot, cold, or warm starts. Be sure to leave the ground-indicating test lead connected so that you may detect intermittent grounds should any occur during this operating check.

REPAIRING

Do not be too eager to dismantle an automatic toaster, but first explore every possibility of making adjustments or learning the cause of failure from the outside. In some models numerous repairs and adjustments can be effected from the bottom after the removal of nothing more than the crumb tray. Furthermore, it is always desirable to learn the cause of failure quickly and especially if appearances denote that repairs may be costly, in which case you will want to quote an estimate before going too far—for customers do not like unpleasant surprises.

4-13. The Key to Skillful Service. When a particular model toaster is taken apart for the first time, however, it is a good idea to take an extra few minutes to study its method of operation and learn thereby the exact purpose of every part. Such an examination not only makes servicing a great deal easier the next time you handle a similar model, but it also enables you to know just how many adjustments and services may be performed without dismantling.

With some models it is possible to put the toaster through its cycle with the shell removed so that you can observe the various parts in actual operation. And there are models whose timing and carriage-latch tripping mechanisms are situated beneath the toaster, directly above the crumb tray. To watch this type of mechanism in operation: first, expose the toaster's underside; then, elevate the toaster 3 or 4 inches with wooden blocks under the corners; next, place a small mirror on the workbench below the mechanism; and finally, aim a flashlight about in line with your vision toward the mirror and you will be able to see everything that is going on.

Always remember to pad the workbench with several thicknesses of soft cloth to prevent scratching the toaster before laying it on its side or turning it upside down, and be sure to keep tools and loose parts away from the padded area.

4-14. Disassembly Precautions.   With the outer shell removed from some models, the bread guide wires are free to drop out when the chassis is inverted.   Such a helter-skelter spilling of these slender rods can do serious damage to other parts of the toaster, for almost invariably some of the guide wires become entangled in one or more heating elements. Always remove the shell with the toaster right side up, therefore.   Then, if the work you propose to do necessitates removal of the guide wires, lift them out one or two at a time.

On the other hand, if you do not need to remove the guide wires, and wish to be spared the time required to reinstall them, fasten them in place by pulling a piece of cellophane tape tautly over the upper ends of each row of guide wires, continuing the tape down the ends of the toaster's inner frame about 2 inches—but be sure to remove the tape before you install the outer shell.

4-15. Probing.   Careful examination in the bread slots from above or below with a flashlight often will disclose the cause of element failure or a ground within the toaster.   For example, you may be able to see the dangling end of a damaged heating element lying against either the carriage or a bread guide wire; and if so, try to move the loose end away from the other parts temporarily—at least long enough to test with the prods to find out if that is the *only* ground. If this temporary measure does eliminate the ground and the series test reveals no short circuits, try heating the toaster just long enough to see if all the other elements heat. (This is the only way to test parallel-connected elements without disconnecting, but if all elements are connected in series, each may be tested separately with the prods without disconnecting.)

If no elements heat—and switch or timer trouble has been ruled out as the possible cause—further examination in the slots may reveal a burned-off connecting wire. This fault, too, in some models can be corrected without dismantling, after which a test of the remainder of the functions may be carried out.

4-16. Cord Sets. These so infrequently require service that they should be replaced, except for the installation of a new attachment plug. See references to cord sets in Chap. 2.

4-17. Switch. In some models, after several years of service, crumbs may collect between the switch contacts in which case step 3 under *Testing* will frequently reveal this fault. Usually, a thorough cleaning of the mechanism will overcome this trouble. But, after cleaning, if the switch does not close properly *every time*, renew the faulty parts.

4-18. Heating Elements. These should never be patched nor any portion of the resistance wire unwound to make slack for reconnecting to a terminal.

When ordering new elements, it is important to note if a rating is stamped on the old element and, if so, to include this information on the purchase order along with the location of the element—that is, center, outside, or any other peculiarities—for in some models the center and outside elements are of unequal resistance; still others may have an opening in one element for the thermostat. Following these precautions will ensure uniform toasting after the installation of new elements.

4-19. Exterior Parts. The base, the control knobs, the handles, and other plastic parts should be examined for possible damage, for if such parts are chipped, cracked, or broken, it is almost a certain indication that the toaster has been dropped and that its interior parts have sustained more serious damage. When appearances lead you to believe that a toaster has been dropped, you should, therefore, scrutinize with more than ordinary care every part and sub-assembly so that you will overlook nothing that is required to restore every function to satisfactory condition.

4-20. Timer Adjustments in General. All timing devices are set at the factory to make medium toast on the *medium* setting of the color control. Erratic operation usually indicates a disjointing of the timer components or some other integral fault, but assuming that all other parts are operating properly, if the bread test reveals that the color control must be turned too close to either extreme for medium toast —and that the color can be varied through the control—the need for an adjustment is quite clear.

Be sure to cool the toaster to room temperature before making timer adjustments and always begin the bread test from a cold start in order to prove the accuracy of your adjustment.

To achieve exact calibration in the shortest time, make the adjustments with extreme care and in minute fractions of an inch.

Consult the manufacturer's service manual for the make in hand for measured clearances of critical adjustments.

4-21. Single-stage Thermostatic Timer Adjustment. In some makes this adjustment can be made from the bottom of the toaster by merely turning a regulating screw; in others, repositioning of the color-control button is all that is necessary. The point to remember, however, is that in this type of timer if the toast is too dark with the color control set at *Medium,* the adjustment you make must shorten the distance the thermostat blade will have to travel to open the switch; if the toast is too light, you must increase the distance. Be careful that you do not bend the bimetallic blade.

4-22. Two-stage Thermostatic Timer Adjustments. These are somewhat similar to the preceding except that the adjustment must cause the bimetallic blade with its auxiliary heater to travel a shorter distance before it closes the auxiliary short-circuiting switch, if the toast is too dark; or a greater distance, if it is too light. Before attempting any adjustments, though, make certain that the auxiliary as well as all other heating elements are operating, as any variation in resistance will alter the time cycle.

4-23. Compensator Adjustments. Only the bread test will disclose whether or not a compensator adjustment is needed. If the first, second, and third successively toasted slices are not almost uniformly browned—and the bread is uniform in texture—an adjustment is recommended, provided, of course, that everything else about the toaster is properly adjusted. But, remember, *compensator adjustments are rarely necessary.*

With a clock-and-compensator mechanism, if the second, third, and fourth slices are darker than the first, the adjustment you make must cause the compensator to act earlier on the clock; if these slices are lighter than the first, the adjustment must cause the compensator to act later.

It is recommended that you do not attempt to adjust compensators used in conjunction with thermostatic timing until after you have studied the service manual for the make in hand.

4-24. Hot-wire Carriage-actuator Adjustment. Before you decide that the hot wire in this type of mechanism needs an adjustment, you must be absolutely certain that everything else is working properly and that no part of the carriage, or any part adjacent to it, is misaligned so as to impede its free movement. Then if the carriage does not rise all the way to the top, you may try a minute adjustment of the hot-wire regulating screw which is accessible from the bottom of the toaster. But remember that a tiny fraction of a turn is usually all that is needed and you must be extremely careful not to impose too great a stress on the wire.

4-25. Hot-wire Latch-tripper Adjustment. If the toaster is equipped with a *Crisper* (or *Melba*) control, turn this knob to the *soft* extreme and again test for popup before deciding that an adjustment of the hot wire is needed.

Now if all other parts are in proper adjustment and the tripping of the carriage latch is so long delayed that the toaster resumes heating before it pops up, *very slight* tightening of the hot wire may be attempted. Do not try to trim the wire nor reshape either eye in the terminal end. Instead, press a forefinger against the wire right near the terminal post, exerting pressure in the same direction as would tighten the terminal nut to hold the existing tension on the wire; then loosen slightly (about a quarter of a turn) the terminal nut and immediately tighten it again. The friction created by tightening the nut will draw just a little more tension on the wire. Be careful not to overdo this adjustment and break the insulator at the center of the wire where the loop passes over the lever.

4-26. Miscellaneous Mechanical Adjustments and Lubrication. Whenever you service a toaster, no matter how trivial the complaint, see to it that all mechanical movements are precisely aligned, accurately adjusted, and lubricated at all points recommended by the manufacturer.

4-27. The Finishing Touch. Make sure that all current-carrying parts are properly supported so that they cannot later come in contact with other parts and cause a short circuit or a ground. Prove the finished job by subjecting it to testing step 6 (Art. 4-12).

QUESTIONS

1. In a toaster equipped with a spring-motored clock timer and thermostatic compensator, what circumstances in testing would reveal to you that the compensator acts too early on the clock?

2. In a model in which the hot-wire principle is used for tripping the carriage latch, what precautions must you take to prevent damage to other parts of the mechanism when tightening the hot wire?

3. In a make which employs the hot-wire principle to actuate the carriage, what other functions must you check thoroughly before deciding that a hot-wire adjustment is required?

4. In a toaster equipped with two-stage thermostatic timing with an auxiliary heater, would the main elements heat if the auxiliary element were burned out? Give the reason for your answer.

5. Why should you be sure to have the toaster right side up as you remove the outer shell from some models?

6. In addition to the make, the model, and the serial number of a toaster, what other information should you furnish the manufacturer when ordering new heating elements?

7. If your test discloses an intermittent ground—that is, one which occurs only when you move the carriage—would you necessarily have to dismantle the toaster to locate the source of the trouble? How would you attempt to find it?

8. If in the course of testing, a toaster seemed to operate

all right after the "shake" test, would you let it go at that? What more, if anything, would you do?

9. Assuming that the customer's statement on the repair tag mentions that the timer doesn't operate properly and that one side of the toaster doesn't heat—if this were a model equipped with a two-stage thermostatic timer with auxiliary heater, it is quite possible that the timer will operate satisfactorily after the inoperative heating elements have been renewed. Do you agree? Give the reason for your answer.

10. In the testing procedure in this chapter you were instructed to have the toaster right side up for all electrical tests. Why?

CHAPTER 5

Mixers

Although there are minor mechanical differences in the various makes of domestic food mixers, a striking similarity in their construction—and particularly in their controls—will work to our advantage in this discussion. Indeed, most of the mixers you will be called upon to service will have the governor-type speed control. The rest will be equipped with either the movable brush holder or some form of variable resistance for speed regulation, and though your assignments will include but a few of these, a brief description of their operating principles is given in Art. 5-3 notwithstanding.

COMPONENTS AND HOW THEY OPERATE

5-1. The Motor. The motor used in nearly all domestic food mixers is the series-type commutator motor.

5-2. The Gear Case. In some makes the gear case contains two worm gears—one for each beater spindle—driven by a worm which usually is formed into one end of the armature shaft. See Fig. 5-1, Items 10 and 13. In other makes, a train of spur or helical gears is employed to accomplish the same purpose, in which case the end of the armature shaft is machined into either a pinion or a coupling. A few models feature three beaters.

As the gear case must be charged with grease, a felt or similar packing washer or seal is used where the spindle shafts emerge from the gear case.

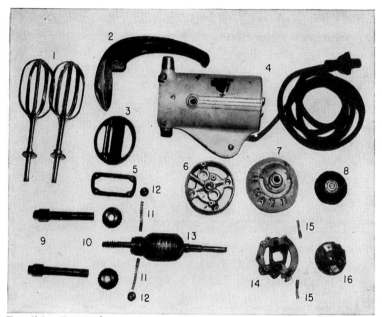

Fig. 5-1. Principal operating parts of one type of mixer motor. Item 1, the beaters; 2, the handle; 3, gear case cover; 4, housing and field assembly; 5, gear case cover gasket; 6, motor end frame (rear); 7, rear housing cap; 8, control dial; 9, spindles; 10, gears; 11, commutator brushes and springs; 12, brush caps; 13, armature; 14, governor brush holder and resistor assembly; 15, governor brushes and springs; 16, governor disc assembly.

5-3. Speed Control. Most of the earlier models were equipped with a three-speed rheostat. Somewhat later, the tapped field and the movable brush-holder methods were introduced. The first two are similar, of course, in that they constitute a variable resistance. The third utilizes the principle whereby the speed of the motor may be varied by slightly rotating the brushes concentrically with the commutator. At least two of these control systems are being used on some of today's fully portable and junior model mixers.

One type of centrifugal governor comprises a set of spring-loaded arms, attached to a hub or disc on the armature shaft, which are gradually impelled outward by centrifugal force as the motor gathers speed. The springs in this type are so designed that the arms do not reach their outer extreme until the motor has attained its full speed. Then, as the motor slows down, the springs pull the arms toward the starting position. Thus, the arms of the governor assume a definite position for every speed variation. For example, the arms will be fully extended at full speed; half, at half speed; one-quarter, at quarter speed, and so on—with proportionate changes in between. This gradual movement of the governor arms is transmitted by mechanical means to the governor switch which is opened and closed intermittently to maintain the speed selected on the control dial. Setting the dial at a lower speed shortens the required travel between the governor-actuating member and the switch; moving the dial to a higher speed increases this travel. There is not, however, a complete cessation of power with these rapid openings of the governor switch. To prevent "bumping" and to reduce arcing at the switch points, a resistor and a condenser are connected in parallel across the governor-switch terminals.

Though all centrifugal governors utilize a similar principle, there is another somewhat different method of operation by which the same purpose is carried out. To state it simply: the governor arms in this type must move to their outer extremes by centrifugal force to open the governor switch at any speed—even the lowest. Speed control is accomplished by varying the pressure on the governor arm spring (or springs) through the control dial. Increasing the pressure obviously forces the machine to run faster in order to throw out the governor arms against this opposing tension, while a very light pressure would cause the motor to creep. Hence, numerous speeds are possible between these two extremes. As in the preceding type, this governor control also requires a resistor and a condenser to prevent pulsating operation which would otherwise be present in all but the highest speed.

Doubtless, you have already gathered that the two distinguishing characteristics of the governor-type speed control are (1) a wide range of speeds, and (2) that the full power of the motor is available at any speed.

5-4. Radio Interference Suppressor. Nearly every make of mixer is now equipped with a radio interference-suppressing condenser which is connected across the line terminals. A third wire leading from this condenser is grounded to the motor body.

5-5. The Beaters. These are locked into the spindles by snap-action (usually ring-and-groove) in many models; in some others, by a yoke and setscrew arrangement. Exact radial positioning is assured by a squared, keyed, or slotted end on the beater shaft which fits into a corresponding socket in the spindle.

5-6. The Beater Ejector. This is a convenient feature on many models using snap-action beaters. This simple mechanism enables the user, by flipping the handle or by pushing a lever, to partially eject the beaters with little effort.

5-7. Juicer. This attachment, consisting of a spouted bowl, a strainer, and a reamer, is usually driven by one of the beater spindles.

5-8. Other Accessories. Other accessories are available by the score, some makes requiring a power unit (an extra gear box for speed reduction and power increase) between the spindle and the accessory. A few brands feature a self-contained auxiliary gear train so that the accessories may be attached directly to the mixer motor.

TESTING

For simplicity—a single, seven-step testing procedure is presented here for all mixers. See Fig. 5-2. And while

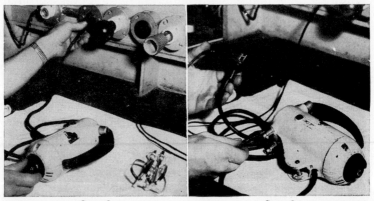

Step 2	Step 3

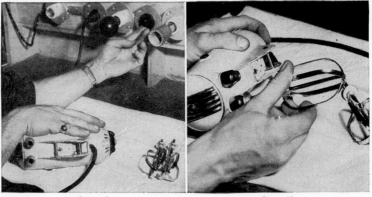

Step 4	Step 5

Fig. 5-2. Testing steps 2 through 7. Visual inspection (not shown) is first. Then, step 2, preliminary continuity test; 3, ground test; 4, closing the 1,000-watt tester-coil switch; 5, attempting to isolate the point of

this plan is primarily intended for mixers equipped with the governor-type speed control, the procedure is easily adapted to models without this feature by merely omitting the references to the governor.

5-9. A Seven-step Test. As emphasized in preceding chapters, it is most desirable to explore first every external analysis to learn the cause of failure before dismantling an appliance—and mixers are no exception. To this end, therefore, we begin the test with a visual examination of the motor assembly. Be sure to pad the workbench surface to protect the finish of the machine, then proceed as follows:

1. Before connecting the motor to the tester, check all these exterior parts for possible damage: handle, control dial, carbon brush caps, beaters, and the beater ejector—if the mixer is so equipped. If the beaters are broken or bent, insert a new set temporarily in order to check the alignment of the spindles. If it appears that the beaters would clash when running, you must, of course, time the spindles to correct this fault before returning the machine to the customer.

Step 6   Step 7

bearing seizure; 6, full-speed running test; 7, final test through all speeds, using a tachometer for precise speed check.

Now look for evidences of oil leaks around the spindle bearings and at the gear-case cover. Make brief notes of every detail as you go along to avoid overlooking any when you do the repair work.

2. Remove the beaters, set the control dial at the highest speed and *leave it there until you reach step* 7. Open the tester-coil switch and connect the mixer cord set to the series test receptacle for the continuity test through a 25-watt lamp. If the test lamp flickers *on and off,* or if it does not light at all, try to isolate the open circuit or loose connection either to the cord set or to the commutator brushes in this manner: stress-test the cord, being careful not to jar the motor; if this does not reveal cord trouble, with one hand hold the motor above the workbench and with the heel of your other hand bump the motor housing near the carbon brush caps. If carbon brushes and/or springs are worn out, this bumping may cause the test lamp to flicker. Replace brushes, springs, or attach a test cord—whichever is necessary to continue the test. If the test lamp *stays on but varies in brilliance* when the motor is shaken endwise, this may indicate either a faulty governor switch or worn-out governor brushes—if the motor under test has governor brushes. (Do not confuse this type of testing flicker with an on-and-off flicker.) However, if all these efforts fail to establish an *unwavering* closed circuit, partially dismantle the motor to the extent necessary to test the internal parts separately. If the test lamp glows steadily, continue as follows:

3. Disconnect the mixer from the series tester and test the motor for grounds with the prods. Be sure to touch one prod to both terminals of the attachment plug and the other to an unpainted metal part of the motor housing. If grounded, remove the commutator brushes and repeat the test, for this will enable you to isolate the ground to one of two general sections—the armature or the rest of the mo-

tor. If this test discloses that the fields, the controls, or the wiring may be grounded, enough of the motor will have to be exposed to test these parts separately. Although the radio interference suppressor is rarely the cause of a ground, you can quickly eliminate this possibility by disconnecting the third wire which runs from this condenser to the motor housing. If the motor is not grounded, proceed as follows:

4. While holding the motor to the workbench padding to prevent its rolling, again connect the mixer cord set to the series test receptacle and close the 1,000-watt tester coil switch. As you flip the tester switch, the lamp should dim considerably and the motor should run at nearly full speed. If it does run freely at full speed, skip step 5. If the motor hums but does not run, or if it labors, this denotes binding and you must *disconnect the cord immediately* to prevent further damage; then continue as follows:

5. To locate the point of binding, jamming, or bearing seizure, insert one beater into a spindle and try turning it a little by hand, first in one direction and then in the other —but do not exert too much force. Now try this same maneuver with the beater in the other spindle, or spindles. If there is very slight free movement—amounting to no more than the play between gear teeth—in the spindles, you have isolated the seizure to the motor. But if one spindle is rigid, obviously, that one is jammed. If any spindle can be turned rather freely to a greater extent than the play between gear teeth, the gear on that spindle either may be stripped or loose on its shaft. If the motor is jammed, expose enough of the interior so that you may try revolving the armature by hand; this will enable you to learn whether the bearings have seized or some part of the armature or its appurtenances are striking a stationary part of the motor.

6. At this stage it is assumed that the armature will rotate freely and that there is a closed circuit within the motor, but no short circuits nor grounds. With the beaters re-

moved, connect the cord set to a power outlet and the ground-indicating lead to the motor housing and run the motor at full speed for a few minutes. Check carefully these five points: irregular speed, overheating, burning odor, smoking, and excessive arcing at the commutator—as any one may indicate a faulty armature, *provided there is no binding in the mechanism and that the commutator and brushes are in good condition*. If the machine responds to this test satisfactorily, continue as follows:

7. With the motor still connected as in step 6, watch the ground-indicating lamp as you test the motor through all the other speeds by gradually turning the control dial from the full speed position all the way to *off*. If there is no speed change near the high or low extreme on the dial, the governor may need regulating. If the motor operates at full speed on all dial settings, including *off*, this indicates a short-circuited governor condenser in many makes; while full speed on all positions except *off* may indicate a stuck governor switch. A pulsating operation in all speeds except *full* usually indicates an open resistor. If there is smooth operation and a speed change at each step, and if the motor stops at the *off* position on the dial, you may be reasonably certain that the machine is functioning properly. For the finishing touch, however, check the highest and lowest spindle speeds with a tachometer and compare the result with the manufacturer's recommended speed in your service manual for the make under test.

PROCURING PARTS

It matters not what your present status is—serviceman or supervisor in the employ of another, self-employed, or student of appliance service—you must be able to choose wisely your sources of supply for parts; for though that responsibility may not be yours already, it may be thrust upon you later. The question "Where to buy parts?" has but one answer—from the appliance-manufacturer's nearest authorized service center. In other words, make it a rule to use genuine parts exclusively on *all* the appliances you service. If you wonder why such a general rule is injected here, it is because the temptation to deviate from it is heightened when one begins the servicing of mixers. The reasons follow.

5-10. Not a Bargain Hunt. In some communities, certain items—such as resistors and condensers of similar specifications to the original—may be available as bulk electrical supplies for a few cents less, and perhaps you can adapt some of these to several makes, but this practice will often lead to butchering and unnecessary additional labor expense. Don't let fancy price lists lure you away from a genuine-parts-exclusively policy.

Bear in mind, too, that no small armature is worth rewinding if a new one is obtainable—whatever the apparent saving. Armature burnouts in mixers are rare, but when you do need a replacement, install a new one with complete assurance that it is *all* new and that it is in perfect balance.

5-11. Miscellaneous Hardware. Your miscellaneous hardware stock should include armature shaft shims for every make you service so that you will not be tempted to improvise these seemingly unimportant parts from unsuitable fiber washer assortments when reinstalling an armature. You will note as you go along that these shims are made from many different materials, such as fiber, spring steel, self-lubricating powdered metal, aluminum, felt, and others. Each has its place and purpose.

5-12. Brushes and Springs. A kit of carbon brushes and springs may be a useful collection in a parts inventory to draw on for patching up obsolete appliances, but do not ever select your mixer brushes or springs from it. The brushes and springs supplied by each manufacturer for his own make are carefully selected to suit the motor for which they are intended. Therefore, with genuine brushes and springs, it is very unlikely that a motor will run on the springs alone after the brushes have worn out. Conversely, if improper brushes and excessively long springs are used, three adverse forces begin a series of damaging effects on the motor: (1) an added frictional load is immediately imposed, (2) abnormally rapid wearing of the commutator, and (3) the excessively long springs will permit the motor to run on the springs alone after the brushes have worn out—resulting, of course, in a ruined armature and possibly other costly damage.

The best investment you can make, therefore, in your customer's behalf—and in your own future—is the replacing of inoperative parts with new, genuine parts.

SERVICING THE MOTOR

5-13. Armature. No electrical appliance is improved by unnecessary dismantling and reassembling, but when you must take a mixer motor apart to the extent that the armature is to be removed, follow these precautions carefully:

Clean the workbench surface and pad it with a *thoroughly clean,* dry cloth. Make certain that there are no fragments of steel wool, grit, filings, or the like anywhere near the work area. If possible, have ready a small, covered, cardboard box in which to put the armature for safekeeping while you are working on the rest of the motor. Place a tray for small parts toward the back of the bench, and lay out your tools to one side of the work area so that nothing will be likely to get under the motor housing and mar the finish. One more thing—lock up your hammer and chisels and give the key to someone else, please.

Now if the armature has responded favorably to testing procedure steps 3 and 6, inspect it immediately on removal from the motor for surface damage and/or faults, such as: loose commutator leads, smoked or uneven commutator, worn or bent shaft, and evidences of burned windings.

A slightly smoked commutator often can be cleaned with a good grease solvent, such as carbon tetrachloride. To do this, make a pad of cloth about the width of the commutator and long enough to encircle it, saturate the cloth with the solvent, then squeeze the pad tightly around the commutator with one hand while you revolve the armature with the other. If this scouring is not effective, cut a strip of very fine sandpaper, 4/0 to 8/0, no wider than the commutator but long enough to encircle it, and repeat the process described above using the sandpaper instead of the cloth. Be careful that the edge of the sandpaper does not touch the windings and that no grit gets into the windings. If the commutator is uneven, however, it will have to be turned down by a machinist.

The armature should be replaced if your inspection reveals loose commutator leads, severely damaged commutator, defective shaft, burned windings, or grounds.

An unbalanced armature, easily detected by violent vibration of the motor at full speed, is an extremely rare fault in food mixers, but every household has an amateur mechanic and when one of these hammer-happy handy men sails into a mixer motor anything can happen! Armature unbalance may be caused by a bent shaft, lost or improperly placed balancing or insulating wedges, improperly positioned or broken governor member and/or cooling fan, or by any other damage which would alter perfect distribution of the weight of the armature. You can, of course, replace some

damaged appurtenances on the armature, but if the armature proper is out of balance you must send it to the factory
for balancing; don't attempt this operation yourself.

Assuming that your tests have revealed that the armature
is all right, clean the shafts by rubbing them vigorously with
a cloth moistened with carbon tetrachloride and put the
armature in a safe place until you are ready to assemble the
motor.

5-14. Bearings. To clean sleeve bearings, tear off a strip
of clean dry cloth about 1×5 inches, saturate it with
carbon tetrachloride, and twist the cloth into a long cylindrical swab, thick enough to fit the bearing snugly. Twirl and
move the swab through the bearing with a seesawing motion.

To test the bearings for transverse and/or vertical wear
and for free movement, insert the armature shaft into one
bearing at a time. Here, you need a discerning touch, for
this is a precision fit where no looseness can be tolerated, but
where free rotating movement is essential. In operation,
worn or elongated bearings cause the motor to chatter,
usually more so when starting and in the lower speeds, but
do not confuse this abnormal sound with that of a noisy
governor.

Food-mixer bearings seldom require replacement, but
when you are confronted with such a job, follow the manufacturer's recommended servicing procedure to the letter.
For example, one manufacturer may suggest sending the
entire motor to the factory for bearing replacement; another
may supply the bearings separately and also have available
at nominal cost the aligning reamer or burnishing tool
which, if required, you must have to fit the bearings correctly; still another may furnish the bearings as a subassembly with the motor end caps ready for use without reaming.

When you do install new bearings, if the service manual for the make in hand does not give complete instructions, you may find this general procedure helpful. First of all, keep in mind that the armature must be perfectly centered between the field magnets where it revolves with extremely close clearance; and—in order to ensure this perfect centering as well as exact alignment, one bearing with the other— not even the slightest deviation in angle can be tolerated. You must, therefore, use the utmost care in handling the end caps, the housing, and other related parts so that you do not unintentionally distort them and thereby render alignment impossible. With these precautions in mind let us assume that the motor is apart and you are ready to replace the bearings.

Clear the work area and put the motor housing or end cap which contains the *worse* bearing in front of you. *Always begin with the worse bearing.* Examine the end cap to find out if anything would hinder removal of the old bearing, such as oil tube or wick or the like, and remove any such parts. Compare the new bearing with the old one to be sure they correspond. Now in order to position the new bearing correctly, note the amount of protrusion of the old bearing on one side or the other; if one side is flush, mark that side of the housing with a crayon if you fear you will forget. If neither side is flush, measure the inside protrusion and record this measurement. If the bearing has a shoulder, it almost invariably faces to the inside. If you do not have a bearing installation tool in your kit, you can easily and quickly improvise one for less than a dollar by following the directions in the next paragraph.

Select from your snap-on socket wrenches the smallest socket into which the mixer motor bearing, including the shoulder (if it has one), will slide easily. See Fig. 5-3. Now try the socket over the protusion of the old bearing to make sure that the socket edges will seat squarely against the boss of the housing. Lacking a better name, we shall call this part of the tool the receiving collar. The rest of the tool comprises a fillister-head cap screw slightly smaller in diameter than the bearing bore and about ½ inch longer than the bearing and the receiving collar combined. A common smooth iron washer, a lead washer, and a hexagon nut to fit the cap screw complete the tool.

Now decide from which side of the housing you will withdraw the bearing; if the bearing has a shoulder, you have no

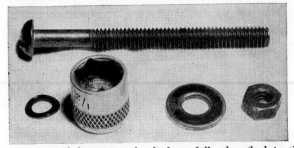

Fig. 5-3. Improvised bearing tool which is fully described in the text.

choice; but if not, remember that the shortest way out is always preferred. Slip the cap screw through the old bearing from one side of the housing, and on the other, fit the receiving collar over the bearing protrusion and onto the boss; while holding these parts loosely in position, put the iron washer and the nut onto the threaded end of the cap screw and draw it up finger-tight, being careful to center the entire rig. Lubricate the washer with a few drops of light machine oil. Now as you tighten the nut with a wrench, the bearing will be drawn slowly into the receiving collar with no risk of distorting the housing. See Fig. 5-4.

To install the new bearing, separate the parts of the improvised tool and slip the lead washer first onto the cap

screw and follow it with the new bearing. We shall not use
the receiving collar at this stage, but to eliminate wobbling
of the cap screw as the new bearing is drawn in, cut off
about ¼ inch from the old bearing to serve as a guiding
collar. File or grind enough from the outside of this collar
so that it can be pushed into the bearing aperture with your

F<small>IG</small>. 5-4. Withdrawing a bearing with the aid of the improvised bearing
tool illustrated in Fig. 5-3.

fingers. If you have a choice as to which side to insert the
new bearing, choose the shortest way in. Note at this point
whether a special radial position of the bearing is required
to coincide with an oil tube or the like.

Now start the bearing with your fingers if possible, but if
not, place it as nearly straight as you can with the cap screw
still in it and the lead washer under the head and slip the
guiding collar over the threaded end of the screw and into
the bearing aperture on the opposite side of the housing,
then put the iron washer and the nut on the screw. Make
sure that the iron washer seats squarely against the boss,
drop a little oil between the nut and the washer, and tighten

finger-tight. Now align the whole arrangement and start tightening it with a wrench, carefully watching the progress of the operation as you do so. Remember, extreme force is not necessary—so go slowly. If the wrench does not turn easily, check the alignment as the bearing may be slightly cocked. When the bearing is about two-thirds in, remove the nut and iron washer so that you can shake out the guiding collar. If the bearing is to be drawn up flush, replace the nut and iron washer and continue tightening. The washer will stop the bearing perfectly flush. If the bearing is to protrude, however, interpose the receiving collar so that you can pull through the protrusion.

In order to preserve as nearly as possible the original alignment of the armature, the next step in the installation of new sleeve bearings is the reaming of the one new bearing just installed—if reaming is required. First, assemble the motor without the armature, tightening the end caps evenly and as firmly as you would for the final assembly; then slide the aligning reamer through the old bearing—which is to serve as a guide for the reamer hub—and into the new bearing, turning and advancing the reamer slowly until the new bearing is reamed. If the other bearing is to be replaced, repeat the installation process using the first new bearing installed as a guide for the reamer for the second bearing. When both bearings are in place and reamed, assemble the motor again, but this time with the armature in order to check the alignment and also to find out how many shims, if any, will be required.

5-15. Fields. When the motor is opened for other service, the field coils are easily tested with the prods in series with a 25-watt lamp. Each coil may be tested separately for open circuits, short circuits, and grounds. *Do not, however, add the 1,000-watt tester coil to the series lamp when testing field coils;* if you are in doubt as to whether there is a closed or short circuit, check the magnetism of the core with a screwdriver while the coil is connected in series with a 25-watt lamp. If either field coil is faulty, replace both. Never attempt to repair defective field coils.

5-16. Commutator Brushes and Springs. If you would rise above mediocrity as a serviceman, remember this small detail: Whenever you service the motor, clean the carbon brush slots thoroughly and make sure that the brushes will slide all the way through under no more pressure than their own weight. If the motor is apart, you can seesaw a swab (similar to that suggested for cleaning bearings) through each slot until it is perfectly clean. If there is evidence of grease in the slots or on the brushes, clip a warning note to the repair tag to remind the service counter attendant to show the customer where the motor *should* be oiled.

5-17. Assembling the Motor. Assuming that all the original parts which you intend to reinstall have been cleaned and neatly spread out together with the new parts, before you begin assembling the motor examine the interior wiring of the housing for proper placement to prevent fouling the armature and make certain that all splices and connections are tight and that each is compactly and adequately insulated.

One of the most important steps in assembling any machine is the providing of initial lubrication for all its moving parts. Put a few drops of oil, therefore, into each bearing and a little on the armature shafts so that lubrication is assured from the first revolution.

As you assemble the housing, push the parts into place with your hands and then check the armature for free movement by twirling the shaft. Now tighten the housing screws gradually, alternating between opposite screws to ensure good alignment, twirling the armature shaft occasionally as you go along. If binding occurs as the ends are drawn up, and you are sure that they are being drawn up evenly, separate the parts, remove one shim, and reassemble. End play adjustment is critical in nearly all mixer motors; too much will cause erratic governor operation; insufficient end play will jam the motor. Do not force the parts together, but take time enough to get this portion of the work as nearly perfect as possible.

The final end-play adjustment in some makes, however, is made from the outside through a thrust-regulating screw and hence can be left until the motor is completely assembled. You must be careful, though, even in this type, that the proper thrust washer, if required, is in place on the opposite end of the armature shaft before you close the motor. To adjust the end play in this model, tighten the thrust-regulating screw just to the point where the armature starts to bind, then back it off about a quarter of a turn and tighten the checknut. Keep in mind the commutator when making end-play adjustments, for you must be sure that the brushes will center upon the running surface of the commutator.

Now make certain that the oil wicks, if required, are in place and that the oil chambers are charged with the oil recommended by the manufacturer.

The cord set is such an inexpensive part of a mixer that it should be replaced if it is faulty in any respect. Examine it for cracked, broken, or gummy outer sheath.

With some makes you may be able to do at least a full-speed running test at this point, but generally it will be less trouble for you to defer a running test until the governor is in place.

SERVICING THE GEAR CASE

5-18. Gears. You must—without exception—clean the gear case thoroughly and discard *all* the old lubricant whenever you install new gears, for it is impossible to rid this enclosure of worn or broken gear fragments in any other way. Remember that one stray chip can do serious damage.

5-19. Clean the Spindle Bearings. Whenever you remove the spindles clean them by the same method as that suggested for motor bearings and clean the spindle shafts with a solvent, then try the shafts in the bearings for free movement without lubricant. Be sure, however, to provide initial lubrication before final assembly of these parts.

5-20. Replace Oil Retainers. Do so whenever you remove the spindles, even though there was no evidence of an oil leak, for once the seals are disturbed it is unlikely that they will be fully effective after reinstallation.

5-21. Alignment of the Spindles. This is not difficult, as most manufacturers provide some obvious means of positioning the gears on the shafts, such as a countersunk setscrew seat in the spindle shaft and/or mating marks on the gears. You can always be sure of exact alignment by trying the beaters in the spindle sockets. After some experience, however, a glance into the sockets as you position the spindles will suffice. Just remember that in nearly all two-beater machines the spindles are timed 45 degrees apart with their indexing pins in this position:/—. In three-beater mixers, the two outer spindles are usually timed parallel with the center beater 45 degrees ahead, like this: —/—.

5-22. When a Spindle Shaft Seizes in Its Bearing. Remove the setscrew from the gear, improvise a wrench from an old beater for extra leverage, and use this tool to twist out the jammed spindle. Flood the spindle shaft and bearing edge with penetrating oil first, though, so that as you work the tight shaft out, oil will follow it into the bearings thereby reducing the force required as you proceed. If you have to force the jammed spindle and its gear part of a revolution against the opposition of the worm in order to gain access to the gear setscrew, you must find out from the manufacturer's service manual *in which direction* to apply such force. When you have removed the spindle, clean it and the bearing, test for free movement, and lubricate as suggested in Art. 5-19.

5-23. Before Closing the Gear Case. Put the right quantity and type of lubricant into it as recommended by the manufacturer, install a new gasket (if one is used), attach the gear-case cover, and clean the outside of the machine.

SERVICING THE GOVERNOR

5-24. Position of Rotating Member. The exact position of a rotating governor member on the armature shaft is extremely important. When this part is fastened with a setscrew, a seat for the setscrew point is usually countersunk into the armature shaft. An easy way to ensure precise positioning is to run the setscrew in only part of the way at first, and then try rocking the governor member slightly on the shaft; if the setscrew has partially entered the seat you should be able to rock the member just a little. Once assured that you have started the screw into the seat, tighten the member firmly. Now revolve the armature by hand to make sure that the governor member does not strike any stationary part of the motor.

5-25. Governor Brushes and Collector Ring. When servicing a governor of this type, clean the collector ring in the same manner as you would a commutator, and replace the brushes and springs if necessary.

5-26. Check the Governor Switch Contacts. Check for free movement, note whether they are burned, and see to it that they close properly. Remember that governor switches which are *normally open* must close *before* the line switch does.

5-27. The Resistor and Governor Condenser. These may be tested separately in series with a 25-watt lamp; the lamp should glow to about half or more of its normal brilliance when the resistor is tested; but the lamp should *not* light when the condenser is so tested.

5-28. Controls. Put a small amount of gear lubricant on the speed-selector dial hub, on its related parts, and a little on the beater ejector wherever there is friction—provided of course that the grease will not get into the electrical components. Attention to this minor detail will assure smooth operation of these parts—but don't overdo it.

5-29. Speed. If it is necessary to regulate the speed, consult the manufacturer's service manual for the recommended speed and for the method of adjustment as these details vary with different makes.

PROVE THE WORK

When finally assembled, test the machine thoroughly through steps 6 and 7 under *Testing*, Art. 5–9.

ADDITIONAL RESPONSIBILITY

This may seem elementary, but your responsibility to a customer does not end with a good repair job, but also includes instructing him in the proper use and care of his appliance whenever you find evidences of abuse. But don't go off the deep end—as so many tradesmen do—with a string of high-flown technical gibberish. Rather, tactfully tell him how to avoid recurrence of trouble without capitalizing on his ignorance of mechanical things. Make him feel as though his lack of care was a natural oversight or a misunderstanding of operating instructions which might possibly have happened to anyone.

At first reading you may feel that this policy will in time reduce your volume of service business—don't believe it! Indeed, experience has proved that this extra consideration for a customer will prompt him to go out of his way to beat a path to your door, with his friends, neighbors, and relatives following not far behind. Furthermore, he will noise abroad that he has found at last a shop where not only do they turn out an expert repair job promptly and at reasonable rates, but also one where they always seem to be greatly concerned with prolonging the life of the repaired appliance.

QUESTIONS

1. If a mixer's governor-switch contacts were stuck in the closed position, how would this fault affect the user's ability to control the speed of the machine?

2. How would the speed control be affected if the governor condenser were short-circuited?

3. What kind of faulty operation would be immediately apparent to you if there were an open circuit in the resistor of a governor-type speed control?

4. If a mixer motor hums but will not revolve when connected across the line, does it necessarily follow that the motor is burned out?

5. Name one fault which would cause a mixer motor to vibrate excessively when running at full speed.

6. Somewhat more than the ideal amount of armature-shaft end play can be tolerated in some motors, but even a slight excess in mixers equipped with a governor-type speed control is objectionable.   Why?

7. It has been emphasized in the text that you should

clean the gear case thoroughly and discard all the old lubricant before replacing worn-out or broken gears. Why is this so important?

8. Name at least one mechanical fault which would cause the beaters to clash.

9. If a mixer motor assembly is jammed, explain how you would attempt to isolate the seizure either to the armature or to one of the spindles without disassembling the motor or gear case.

CHAPTER 6

Roasters

If the preceding chapters have given you the impression that complexities in small-appliance servicing multiply as we go along, take heart in the thought that we have arrived at something simpler. Indeed, the test to locate faults in an inoperative roaster can be executed almost invariably without dismantling. Moreover, removal of nothing more than the bottom cover of most models will expose the interior when this is necessary to complete a stage of testing or to renew a part.

COMPONENTS

6-1. Electrical Parts. These comprise a group of heating elements, one encircling the sides of the liner, and one or two beneath it; a thermostat—to maintain an even temperature—which may be varied by the user through the control knob to suit the cooking operation; a pilot lamp on most makes which indicates whether the power is on or off; a cord set; and, in some models, a timer. A broiler unit is available for several makes and is used with the roaster body, but may not be connected simultaneously with the roaster elements because of the severe overload that the two devices would impose upon an ordinary residential convenience outlet circuit. This accessory is used whenever it is desirable to have the heat source above the food.

6-2. Other Principal Parts. These include the liner, the insulation, a top cover, and an outer jacket. The outer jacket is enough larger than the liner to allow space for insulation between the sides of the jacket and the liner and also beneath it. The top cover in some models is unattached; in others, hinged. Most hinged-cover models feature a linking mechanism and operating knob for opening and closing the cover, making handling of the hot cover unnecessary. The large roasting pan, which fits loosely into the liner, can be easily lifted out for cleaning. The rest of the utensils and racks need no description.

TESTING

Hitherto, we have been concerned with protecting the finish of chromium-plated and painted appliances during service operations, but with roasters we have not only the two finishes just mentioned, but also porcelain enamel—which actually is glass bonded to metal. Therefore, clean the workbench surface thoroughly, pad it adequately, and make sure that neither tools nor loose parts get under the roaster.

6-3. A Six-step Test. In order to facilitate turning the roaster during the testing process, remove all loose racks and utensils, including the large roasting pan and the cover, and put these parts on another table out of your way. Now you should have just the roaster body and the cord set on the bench. Use the same series tester as that suggested for other appliances and proceed in the following manner.

1. Inasmuch as virtually all roaster cord sets may be detached by withdrawing the terminal plug from the roaster,

disconnect the cord and test it separately. (See Art. 2-1.) If it is faulty, substitute a test cord and continue as follows:

2. If the roaster under test has a timer, make sure that its controls are so set that it will not interrupt the circuit. Now turn the thermostat dial to the highest temperature and connect the roaster to the series test receptacle. If the roaster does have a timer and the test lamp does not light, you may want to assure yourself at this point that the timer is not at fault by exposing its terminals and short-circuiting them. If the test lamp still does not light, you must expose enough of the interior of the roaster in order to test the thermostat and elements separately with the prods.

If the test lamp does light, close the 1,000-watt tester-coil switch; the lamp should dim to about half its normal brilliance; if it does not, there is a short circuit within the roaster and you will have to open it for separate testing of the internal parts; if the lamp does dim, continue as follows:

3. Revolve the control dial from one extreme to the other as you watch the test lamp to make sure that no "off spots" occur on the scale where they shouldn't. Don't be too critical, however, right near the *off* marking, for these extremely low temperatures are rarely—if ever—used; but if there is not an unwavering closed circuit from about 200 degrees and up, you should include a new thermostat in your list of parts required. Furthermore, if the thermostat is faulty in this respect, you may conclude the preliminary test with step 4, deferring steps 5 and 6 until you have replaced the thermostat.

4. If convenient, connect the ground-indicating lead to some unpainted metal part of the roaster body. If this is not practicable, disconnect the roaster long enough to do a ground test with the prods, but be sure to touch one prod to *both* terminals of the roaster circuit and the other to an unpainted metal part of the roaster body. See Fig. 6-1.

Revolve the control knob from one extreme to the other as you make the ground test. If the roaster is grounded, expose enough of the interior to locate the fault. If it is not grounded, continue as follows:

5. (This step may be omitted when testing several makes. See footnote.*) Assuming that the roaster has responded

Fig. 6-1. Preliminary ground test. If it is impossible to attach the ground-detector lead to the roaster body, use the prods for this test.

favorably to all the preceding tests, set the control dial at any *on* position, connect the roaster cord set to a power outlet, and *immediately*—before it gets hot—place the palms of your hands flat against the bottom of the liner to find out

---

* Although many makes have the one side element connected in series with a single bottom one, some are equipped with two bottom elements connected in parallel, while this bottom pair is connected in series with the side unit. Therefore, if you want to omit this touch test on all series-connected roasters, check the manufacturer's manual for the make under test to determine if any elements are parallel connected. Obviously, if the roaster has only two elements and these are series connected, neither will heat if either is burned out.

Fig. 6-2. Touch test to determine whether the sides and bottom are heating equally. If this test is used, it must be done immediately after connecting to line voltage.

Fig. 6-3. The temperature test.

whether the entire bottom is heating, then gingerly touch the sides of the liner to make sure that the side element is heating at approximately the same speed. See Fig. 6-2.

6. If you haven't a separate oven tester, use the same temperature meter as that suggested for testing irons by disconnecting the iron-testing stand cable from the meter and attach in its place the oven-testing cable. Improvise some means to support the cable terminal near the center of the inside of the roaster, then lay the cable as flat as possible over the edge of the roaster so that you can close the cover. See Fig. 6-3. Test at 400 degrees and allow the thermostat to cycle at least twice to compensate for possible overshooting on the first shutoff before you make a decison regarding the accuracy of the thermostat. If possible, have the ground-indicating lead attached while making the temperature test, but if you cannot attach the lead, touch it to the roaster several times while it is heating to determine whether or not there are intermittent grounds.

SERVICING

6-4. The Side Element. This is fastened to the liner by several methods; in some makes, it is tied in place with asbestos tape; in some others, it is cemented to the liner; while another manufacturer provides supporting clips on the liner for this purpose; still another may employ some combination of the foregoing.

A few manufacturers will recommend that you send the liner—some, even the entire roaster body—to the factory service station for side-element replacement. Others will supply this element separately together with the related parts and materials required for this operation.

When you are confronted with a side-element burnout, therefore, consult the manufacturer's service manual *before* you remove the faulty element to find out what service procedure applies to that make and model.

When you do intend to replace a side element yourself, be sure that you have everything on hand that you will need for the job *before you begin*—such as asbestos tape, waterglass, or whatever—in order to avoid unnecessary handling of the element, the connecting wires, and the insulation. The specific manual for the make in hand will tell you what miscellaneous supplies are needed for side-element replacement.

6-5. The Bottom Element(s). This element is relatively simple to replace, for it is laid flat against the bottom of the liner and usually can be reached by merely removing the bottom cover and the lower insulation bat. See Fig. 6-4. Be sure to use the installation process recommended by the manufacturer.

6-6. Element Leads. In some instances these may be slightly trimmed if necessary. Though this practice is seldom recommended for other heating appliances, in roasters it is quite often possible to trim approximately ½ inch from an element lead for the purpose of reconnecting when the lead has burned off at a terminal or splicing point. This trivial shortening of the lead will have little or no effect upon the resistance value of the element—and the saving in repair charges to the customer is quite obvious. *Under no circumstances, however, attempt to pull additional length for the lead from the element proper.*

6-7. Interior Wiring. Make and insulate splices in the same manner as originally done by the manufacturer. Do not improvise connecting wires from bulk supplies, but always use the wire supplied by the manufacturer. Be sure that every splice and connection is *tight*. Preserve as nearly as possible the original placement of the wires, being especially careful that the bottom cover screws, when driven in, will not puncture the insulation on the wires or on the splices. See to it that no wires will be pinched when the bottom cover is installed and that none lie against the raw edges of metallic cross members.

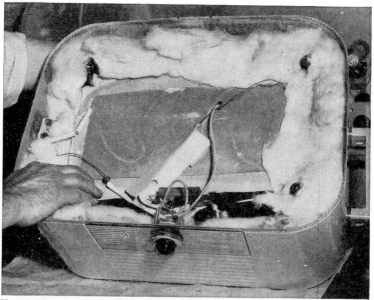

Fig. 6-4. Bottom view with lower cover plate and insulation bat removed to show the lower heating element. (Resistance wires are concealed between sheets of asbestos.)

6-8. Thermostat. When you service a thermostat, remember that heat must be conducted from the liner to the thermostat. For this reason some part of the thermostat must be in direct physical contact with the liner. See Fig. 6-5. Hence, if the thermostat is improperly positioned the roaster may overheat.

On the other hand, if the side element loosens, slips down, and rests upon the thermostat, the power will be shut off by the thermostat long before the selected temperature is reached. Whenever there is a radical malfunction of the thermostat, therefore, before you conclude that an adjustment or a replacement is required, examine the roaster body for exterior damage which might have been caused by accidental dropping, as a shock of this kind usually will derange the internal parts.

6-9. Thermostat Calibration. Some roaster thermostats are provided with a calibrating device, some are not. Lack-

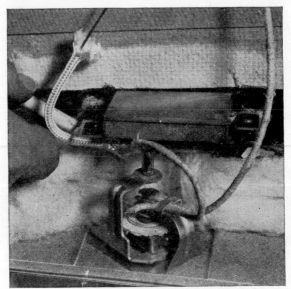

Fig. 6-5. The thermostat, shown here to the right of the serviceman's thumb, must be in direct contact with the liner.

ing specific information, you may find helpful this general procedure for ascertaining the need for adjustment or replacement as you run a temperature test.

If the customer has not complained of inaccurate temperatures, it is most unlikely that you will be able to improve the calibration of the thermostat unless the mean temperature is more than 25 to 35 degrees above or below that which is called for on the dial. For example, say you are testing with the dial set at 400 degrees and the meter shows that the shutoff point is actually 460 degrees and the turn-on point is 380 degrees; you may average these two figures to arrive at a mean temperature of 420 degrees. As pointed out above, if the customer has not complained of temperature inaccuracy, you may presume that the thermostat is all right, for this is not a hair-splitting adjustment. But if the customer *has* complained—in this instance of overheating—make the necessary adjustment or replace the thermostat, as the case may be. Except for calibrating, no other service should be attempted on thermostats.

6-10. Pilot Lamps. Keep one flashlight cell on your bench to use for testing these low-voltage lamps individually and you can distinguish between socket or lamp failure in a matter of seconds.

6-11. The Timer. If inoperative it should be replaced, exchanged, or sent to the factory for service. Ascertain first the manufacturer's recommended service procedure for the make in hand.

6-12. Broiler Unit. Infrequently you may be called upon to replace the open-coil heating element in this accessory. When you receive the new element from the factory, you will find that it is compressed as a closed coil spring and a great deal shorter than the old element. It is your responsibility to stretch the new coil to the correct length immediately before installation. To do this, remove the old coil and measure its length accurately, then stretch the new coil *evenly* to somewhat less than this measure so that when you thread it through the insulating bushings the coil will be under slight tension. To stretch the coil evenly throughout its entire length, fasten one end of it to the workbench and exert the pulling force only at the other extreme end. See Fig. 6-6. If you inadvertently overstretch the new coil, you can correct the error in this manner: Slide the coil onto a piece of drill rod slightly smaller in diameter than the internal diameter of the coil, and then compress it the desired amount on the rod, exerting force only at the extreme ends of course. Be sure to replace any broken insulating bushings before installing the new coil.

6-13. The Terminal Pins. These should be clean and bright to ensure a good electrical connection. If you can

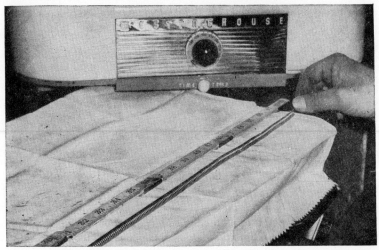

Fig. 6-6. Stretching an open-coil broiler element.

clean these parts satisfactorily with an abrasive, do it; but if not, replace them. Inspect the pins thoroughly, particularly if the terminal plug on the cord set is burned.

6-14. The Cord Set. This should be replaced if it is faulty in any respect, for the nominal price of this item, completely assembled, renders any expenditure for patching sheer false economy.

6-15. Insulation. Distribute the insulation evenly, being careful not to pack it tightly and thereby lessen its effectiveness.

6-16. Porcelain Enamel. When working with porcelain enamel, use only your hands to fit the parts precisely into their proper positions without springing, prying, bending, pounding, or forcing, and tighten the supporting screws *moderately*—never extremely tight. Be sure to use the original or new resilient washers under nuts or screw heads which are to be drawn up against porcelain enameled parts.

6-17. Hinged Cover Models. If necessary, adjust the dial and linking mechanism to ensure smooth, easy operation.

6-18. Miscellaneous Parts. Always check the handles, dials, feet, and so forth, and if any of these are damaged or lost, replace them.

6-19. Prove the Work. Subject the roaster to testing step 6.

QUESTIONS

1. If the series tester indicates intermittent continuity as you move the roaster's temperature control dial between 250 and 275 degrees, would you say that this fault warrants renewal of the thermostat?

2. Thermostats sometimes overshoot the selected temperature on the first automatic cutoff. How can you compensate for this irregularity in making a temperature test?

3. Disregard overshooting for this question and assume that you are testing a roaster with its control dial set at 400 degrees. Would you attempt to improve the calibration of its thermostat if it shuts off automatically at 425 degrees and turns on at 385?

4. How would you test for possible intermittent grounds during the operating test if you could not find a suitable place on the roaster to attach the ground-detector lead?

5. It is explained in the text that you may trim a little

from a roaster's element lead if necessary for reconnecting to a terminal. If the lead is then too short, would you attempt to pull additional length from the element proper?

6. If a roaster's thermostat were improperly positioned so that heat could not be conducted from the liner to the thermostat, what kind of faulty operation would result?

7. Explain how you would obtain the right measure in order to stretch to the desired length a new, coiled-type element for a roaster's broiler unit.

8. Should the insulation be packed tightly between the liner and the outer jacket?

CHAPTER 7

Coffee Makers and Percolators

Undoubtedly the small-appliance service business affords more extra compensations—both to the serviceman and to

Fig. 7-1. Three basic types of coffee-making appliances are, left to right, a nonautomatic percolator, an automatic percolator, and an automatic metal-bowl coffee maker.

his employer—than any other mechanical trade. For example, if scheduled completion dates on appliances in process permit, you can repair percolators in the early morning and then run the "live" tests about 10 A.M.; thus at the appointed time you'll have all the fixings for that respected institution—The Ten O'Clock Coffee Break.

The rewards, however, come at the end of a year when you will be about $62.50 ahead that you didn't spend at the restaurant. Moreover, you can bask in the warmth of the boss's smile when he shares with you the profit-and-loss statement of your department, for it will show approximately $200 more in the black as a result of uninterrupted production—those quarter-hours do add up.

But let's get back on the right track and see how these coffee-making appliances operate. Three basic types are illustrated in Fig. 7-1.

PERCOLATOR COMPONENTS

7-1. Electrical Parts. These comprise a heating element, a cord set, and—in nearly every nonautomatic make and model—a *heat* fuse which serves to prevent damage to the pot from overheating by interrupting the circuit if the percolator should boil dry. In addition to the foregoing parts, automatic models feature a timer, some of which are variable and include a *keeps hot* control.

7-2. The Principal Mechanical Parts. These are the tube (or stem), usually fitted with a valve at the bottom; the coffee basket; and the basket cover (or spreader). Other mechanical parts warrant no description.

PERCOLATOR OPERATING PRINCIPLE

7-3. Nonautomatic. A point of interest is the advantage that the electric percolator has over the ordinary type which needs an outside heat source. In virtually every electric model, a small well or chamber is provided at the bottom of the pot into which the valve (of the valve and stem assembly) is fitted. In operation, the small quantity of water in the well boils almost immediately because the heat is concentrated directly in, under, or around the well. The pressure thus created by the boiling water in the well rap-idly increases until it closes the valve so that for the moment no more cold water will enter this small chamber. With the valve closed, and the only outlet being through the stem, the rising pressure forces the small amount of water up through the stem. Then, as the stem is emptied, the pressure recedes which allows the valve to open again and admit another small quantity of water and the cycle is re-peated. The electric percolator, therefore, begins to per-colate almost immediately after it is connected, while the nonelectric type will not percolate until all the water in the pot has been brought close to the boiling point.

7-4. Fully Automatic Percolators. These are intended to (1) time accurately the brewing cycle which may be varied through the control to suit the taste of the user, (2) keep the finished coffee at a suitable serving temperature without repercolating, and (3) enable the user to reheat the coffee, also without repercolating.

Obviously, space limitations will not permit a detailed description of every automatic percolator mechanism, but an outline of the functions of one type will make it easier to understand the others, most of which are relatively simpler.

One manufacturer employs three elements, a pilot lamp, and two thermostat switches to achieve fully automatic op-eration. Two elements rated at 400 watts each—one for the pump and the other as a booster—are connected in par-allel with the line and are controlled by the two thermostat switches. The third element, rated at 55 watts, is con-nected in series with the pilot lamp and in parallel with the pump thermostat switch. Thus, the 55-watt keeps-hot element and the pilot lamp are connected in series with the pump element when the thermostat switch is open.

When this percolator is cold, however, and the control is set for *mild, medium,* or *strong,* both thermostat switches are closed which short-circuit the pilot lamp and the keeps-hot element and connects both 400-watt elements in parallel. During this first stage of timing, therefore, the temperature of the water rises rapidly and percolation begins almost immediately. This stage of timing ends when the booster element is shut off by its thermostat, but percolation continues in the second stage with only the 400-watt pump element in the circuit. A little later, the pump thermostat switch opens and percolation stops. Now with both switches open, the pilot lamp, the 55-watt keeps-hot element, and the 400-watt pump element are all connected in series and furnish enough heat to keep the coffee at a suitable serving temperature.

Moving the control knob from *mild* to *strong,* in this model, raises the shutoff temperature of the pump thermostat, but at the same time lowers the shutoff temperature of the booster thermostat. If this seems confusing at first glance, bear in mind that the pump element alone produces sufficient heat for percolation, but by the addition of the 400-watt booster element, heat capacity for the initial stage is doubled for a quick start. Now it should be clear that if the booster is cut out of the circuit earlier (at a lower temperature) in the cycle, more time will be required for the pump element to attain its cutoff temperature; hence, a longer percolation period and stronger coffee. On the other hand, if the booster is cut out later (at a higher temperature), the pump element will attain its cutoff temperature in a shorter time and milder coffee will be the result. In the reheat position, this control is so designed that the pump thermostat switch remains open.

VACUUM-COFFEE-MAKER COMPONENTS

7-5. The Principal Parts. The principal parts of the vacuum-type coffee maker consist of the heating unit, the cord set, the lower bowl, the upper bowl with its gasket, the filter, and—on the automatic models—the thermostatic controls.

The nonautomatic glass-bowl domestic models may be regarded as electric appliances only because they are sold with a one- or two-burner table stove, for many housekeepers will continue to use the coffee maker on their kitchen ranges if the glass bowls outwear the electric table stove. Some of these stoves feature two-heat manual control, a high heat for brewing, and a low heat for keeping the brewed coffee warm; others have been manufactured with a simple single heat unit.

At least one manufacturer has produced a fully automatic glass-bowl coffee maker, which to be automatic in operation must be used with the same type of table stove as was originally supplied with the set. This model features a thermostatic control for keeping the brewed coffee warm and a magnetic switch to shut off the high heat at the end of the brewing cycle.

The heating unit and the controls in the metal-bowl models are of course an integral part of the lower-bowl assembly.

VACUUM OPERATING PRINCIPLE

7-6. The Brewing Principle. The brewing principle of all vacuum-type coffee makers is similar. When water is boiled in the sealed lower bowl the pressure thus generated forces all but a small quantity of the water up through the upper bowl spout and thence into the upper bowl into which the proper amount of dry coffee has been previously placed. A partial vacuum is thereby drawn in the lower bowl, for water and steam have been expelled but no air has entered. This vacuum is further intensified when the heat is turned off, for as the lower bowl cools, the remaining vapor condenses, the residue of water—if any—cools and shrinks in volume, and finally the brewed coffee is pulled through the filter and into the lower bowl.

7-7. Glass-bowl Automatic Control. This is the control principle of one type of glass-bowl automatic coffee maker: Assume that both bowls are in place with water in the lower and dry coffee in the upper and that the table stove is connected. At this point the low-heat element, the high-heat element, the thermostat switch, and the pilot lamp are all connected in series. Now when the starting button is depressed, the (magnetic) starting switch is closed thereby short-circuiting the low-heat element and the pilot lamp which allows the high-heat element to heat to its full capacity.

Before proceeding further, it should be understood that in this model a part of the starting switch mechanism is fitted into the lower end of the upper-bowl spout. This part consists of a loose-fitting piston on whose lower end is a metal disc which ordinarily rests of its own weight against the bottom of the lower bowl. This disc serves as an armature to which the Alnico magnet is attracted and held when it is raised manually by depressing the starting button.

A side vent hole is provided in the bowl spout just below the piston head so that when water first begins to rise up the spout, the pressure is nearly equalized above and below the piston, but when the water level in the bowl falls below the vent hole, some steam and air escape to the upper bowl and the boiling rate of the remaining small quantity of water is increased to the point where some of it is driven up the spout with sufficient force to lift the piston and its armature from the field of the magnet, whereupon the magnet drops of its own weight and opens the switch. This switch will remain open until the starting button is again depressed.

The thermostat now takes over control of the stove and when the brewed coffee is drawn into the lower bowl, the low-heat element controlled by the thermostat will keep the coffee at a suitable serving temperature (165 to 185 degrees).

7-8. Metal-bowl Automatic Control. There is a similarity in the control principle of all metal-bowl automatic coffee makers in that two temperatures are required: one for brewing and the other for keeping the finished coffee hot. One manufacturer may use only one heating element, another may use two (high and low), but whether one or two elements are used, the control of the two temperatures is centered in the thermostat.

In one make metal-bowl automatic coffee maker, when the control is set at *low*, the thermostat will maintain a temperature of the coffee in the lower bowl at 165 to 185 degrees. This is a good serving temperature but not hot enough to force the brew up to the upper bowl.

When the lever is latched at *high* to start this model coffee maker, the cutoff temperature of the thermostat is raised considerably so that even after the water has begun to boil, the element will continue to heat until the water has been forced into the upper bowl. At this stage—with little or no water remaining in the lower bowl—the temperature rises with much greater rapidity, whereupon the thermostat trips the latch and a spring returns the lever to *low* where it will remain until it is moved manually. Minor details in structure may vary with different makes, but the basic operating principle is essentially the same.

TESTING

7-9. A Five-step Test.   This procedure will serve for all coffee-making appliances, automatic and nonautomatic. After you have cleared and padded the work area, make a

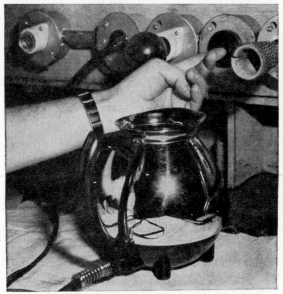

Fig. 7-2.   When the 1,000-watt tester-coil switch is closed, the series lamp should dim; if not, a short circuit is indicated.

careful visual examination of the appliance for surface damage and/or faulty exterior parts and continue as follows:

1. Test the cord set as a separate unit as recommended in Art. 2-1.   If it is faulty, continue with a test cord.

2. With the 1,000-watt tester-coil switch open, connect the appliance to the series test receptacle and, if it is an automatic model, set the control at the highest point.   Make sure that the cord terminal-plug contacts fit the terminals well.   Now if the series test lamp lights, close the 1,000-watt tester-coil switch, but reopen it immediately.   See Fig.

7-2. When you closed the switch, the lamp should have dimmed to a little less than half its normal brilliance. If the lamp did not light at all, you must expose the interior parts for separate testing with the prods. When you connected the appliance, if the lamp lit but did not dim when you closed the 1,000-watt tester-coil switch, a short circuit

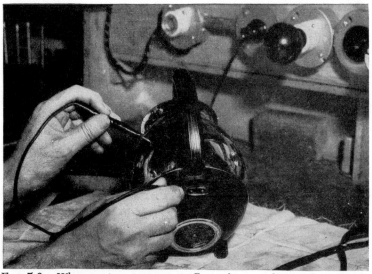

Fig. 7-3. When testing automatic coffee-making appliances for grounds with the prods, make this test with the control in all positions.

is indicated and you must correct this fault before going further. If you are testing a nonautomatic appliance, omit step 3; if automatic, and it responds favorably to this test, continue as follows:

3. Repeat the tests suggested in step 2 with the control in all the other *on* positions, such as *reheat, mild, medium, strong,* or *high* and *low.* Note, however, that when you close the 1,000-watt tester-coil switch momentarily, the test lamp may appear to go almost entirely out on *low* if the ap-

pliance has a very low-wattage keeps-hot element—but this is normal.

4. Test for grounds with the prods; if an automatic model, make this test with the control in all positions.   See Fig. 7-3.

5. In most cases the final test may be made with water alone and you can compare the time values with the manu-

Fig. 7-4.   Here the coffee maker is connected to a power outlet, which is equipped with a pilot lamp, for the heat test.   Note the ground-detector lead attached to the rim of the metal bowl.

facturer's recommendations.   Inasmuch as the thermostat parts move as the heat rises, attach the ground-indicating test lead to all automatic coffee-making appliances to be sure there are no intermittent grounds.   See Fig. 7-4.

SERVICING IN GENERAL

The service notes under this head are common to both percolators and coffee makers.

7-10. Cord Set.   New, complete cord sets are so low in price that no labor expenditure for patching is warranted. To avoid the possibility of springing the terminals or damaging the terminal guard, use only genuine cord sets.

7-11. Terminal Pins.   These must be clean and bright to ensure a good electrical connection.

7-12. Interior Wiring.   All connections must be tight as in any other heating appliance.   Provide safe clearance between exposed live parts and between these parts and the body of the appliance, and preserve as nearly as possible the original arrangement of the wiring.

7-13. Feet.   Check these parts to make certain that they are intact and securely fastened, for a serious accident may result if the appliance tips over.

7-14. Handle.   Inspect the handle supports and screws so that there is no danger of loosening and subsequent flipping over of the appliance when it is picked up.   Use extreme care, however, in tightening the handle band around the neck of a glass coffee maker bowl; excessive force here may break the bowl, particularly if unintentional misalignment of the collar conveys such force directly to the glass.

SERVICING PERCOLATORS

7-15. Fuse.   When the continuity test discloses an open circuit in a nonautomatic percolator, always check first the fuse as this part can be tested in seconds by merely removing the bottom cover.   A quick method of testing a screw-in type fuse is to try tightening it first and then test again, for softening of the cylindrical fuse member will cause the fuse to loosen.   If this test proves that the fuse is faulty in this or in any other respect, replace it with a new one.   If the percolator does not respond to this test, or if it is equipped with any other type of fuse, short-circuit the fuse terminals momentarily in order to rule out fuse trouble. But never return a percolator to a customer with a short-circuited fuse holder—not even as a temporary servicing measure.

7-16. Element. Before attempting to replace a heating element, consult the manufacturer's service manual to determine what else, if anything, you will need to do the job. For some makes you may have to order related parts along with the element, such as gaskets, spacers, or the like. Although in many makes the installation of a new heating element is relatively simple and can be done with ordinary tools, for a few models you would need special tools to do this work satisfactorily. Percolator element burnouts are so rare, however, that in a small shop it would hardly pay to buy this special equipment if it is costly unless you expect to service a large volume of one make. For example, if you repair mixed brands and your volume of business amounts to, say, thirty to forty traffic-appliance service transactions weekly, you may not have more than two or three percolator-element failures a year. It would seem advisable, therefore, to farm out to your authorized service station the infrequent-element replacement jobs for which costly special equipment is needed—at least until experience dictates otherwise.

Always replace a faulty element with a new one. This point cannot be overemphasized, for in automatic percolators particularly, trimming of the element leads may alter the resistance values and thereby render accurate timing extremely difficult, if not impossible.

7-17. Automatic Controls. Before concluding that an adjustment or a replacement of the control is required, be sure that every other part of the percolator is in good working order and that the operating instructions are being followed. When you are assured that the controls are at fault, study the manufacturer's service manual for the make in hand and follow those directions carefully. Automatic percolators vary so widely in design with different manufacturers that no general directions for regulating would be of any value. Suffice it to say that these are exacting adjustments, some of which are measured with inexpensive feeler gauges, and you will save time by avoiding any trial-and-error adjustments.

7-18. Valve and Stem Assembly. This assembly should be carefully inspected for clogging, disintegration, distortion, binding of the valve member, and for any other damage. Make sure that the pump seats properly in the well, but that it does not jam there so that the customer cannot remove it. No attempt should be made to repair this part; if it is faulty in any particular, replace the entire assembly.

7-19. Basket and Spreader. Little attention is needed here, except to note that the basket rests in its proper position on the stem and that the spreader fits the basket.

7-20. Cover and Glass Knob. The glass knob should fasten snugly into the cover. The cover must fit the pot tightly enough so that it will not fall off when the percolator is tilted for pouring. These adjustments are so simple they warrant no detailed discussion, but one word of caution: don't buy your replacement glass knobs from the ten-cent store; rather order them as well as all other parts from your nearest authorized service station.

7-21. Pot. In most cases, no attempt should be made to straighten a bent pot. Instead, send it to a factory-authorized service station where special equipment will be used for this kind of operation.

If a customer wants a pot replated—and the purchase price of the percolator warrants such an expenditure—find out first whether or not the manufacturer will do it; some will suggest that you have this sort of work done locally. Be sure to get an estimate beforehand, in any case.

SERVICING VACUUM COFFEE MAKERS

7-22. Element. One make of domestic coffee-maker stove is so simple in construction that by removing a single screw from the center hole of the heating-unit brick, the brick, coils, and terminal assembly may be lifted out as a single unit. In view of the nominal cost for this entire assembly, it would be false economy to spend time installing a new coil in one of these bricks.

When you have to renew heating elements in other open-coil domestic coffee-maker stoves, it is a good idea to check your price lists to find out whether or not the old brick is worth reusing even though it looks sound. If you can buy the bricks and coils assembled for a few cents more than the coils only, it would be a waste of labor in this case, too, to thread a new coil into the old brick.

Elements for the all-metal coffee makers are handled in a somewhat different manner, most of which you will be able to install yourself with little or no difficulty and without special tools. Consult your manufacturer's manual for complete directions for the make in hand. As in percolators, element failures in all-metal coffee makers are extremely rare. If your shop is in the thirty-to-forty service transactions weekly group, you may average less than one element failure a year.

7-23. Automatic Controls. The need for adjustment or replacement of the controls is more quickly recognized in coffee makers than in percolators. Again, however, you must be sure that all the other parts are in good working order and that the instructions are being followed.

Usually, if the brew does not remain in the upper bowl long enough, this would indicate that the high-heat control shuts off too soon, or vice versa. The manual for the specific make will tell you the length of this period which varies with different brands. If the brew returns to the upper bowl while the control is on the keeps-hot setting, the low-heat control is set too high. The accuracy of this adjustment is easily checked with a hot-water thermometer after heating water in the lower bowl until it has attained its highest temperature with the control in the low-heat posi-

FIG. 7-5. The low-heat temperature test. Observe that the serviceman has improvised a wire support through the ring at the top of the thermometer so that it may be suspended in the water. If the tip of the thermometer rested on the bottom of the bowl, the reading would be inaccurate.

tion. See Fig. 7-5. As previously explained this temperature should be approximately 165 to 185 degrees. Obviously, if the fluid approaches the boiling point it will rise to the upper bowl. If it falls much below the minimum temperature, the coffee would not be hot enough to suit the average coffee drinker. These are minute adjustments and time will be saved if they are made in accordance with the manufacturer's recommendations. In order to avoid the accumulation of excessive labor charges during these heat-up and cool-off periods between adjustments, always have another appliance at hand to work on instead of just waiting.

7-24. Bowls. Follow the same procedure as that suggested for percolator pots when servicing damaged coffee-maker bowls. Remember, too, that where the two bowls are fitted together the contour of each must coincide, as the gasket cannot compensate for a dent.

7-25. Gasket. There must be a good seal at this point, and for that reason inspect the bowl gasket and replace it if it is not perfect.

7-26. Filter. If the coffee maker is equipped with a perishable filter, install a new one to give the finished job a clean, neat appearance.

PROVE THE WORK

Run an operating test as suggested in step 5 at least twice from a cold start. As previously pointed out, this is not a time-consuming operation. Simply place the appliance under test close to the backboard at one end of the work-bench and arrange the cord set and ground-indicating test lead so that they do not cross your work area; then go ahead with the next job. When the final tests have been completed, dry and clean the appliance and it is ready to go.

QUESTIONS

1. Though *Testing*, step 4, recommends that you test all coffee-making appliances for possible grounds with the prods, you are instructed also to use the ground detector particularly on automatic models during the operating test (step 5). Why?

2. Feet and handles are nonoperating parts, of course, yet it is extremely important that these items be intact and securely fastened.   Why?

3. In the course of testing a nonautomatic percolator, it is a convenience to short-circuit a burned-out heat fuse in order to continue the test.   But if you had not the right-style fuse in stock for immediate replacement, would you return to a customer a percolator with a short-circuited heat fuse as a temporary measure so that she could use the appliance pending receipt of the new part?

4. Why is it inadvisable to trim the element leads of an automatic percolator?

5. Before deciding that an automatic percolator's timing mechanism needs adjustment, you must establish two facts. One of these is that every other part of the appliance is operating properly.   What is the other?

6. After the water has risen to the upper bowl in an automatic coffee maker, what fault would cause the brew to be drawn into the lower bowl too soon?

7. What fault would cause the brew to return to the upper bowl while the control is set at *low?*

8. Explain how you would do a low-heat temperature test on an automatic coffee maker.

9. Why is it so essential to satisfactory operation to have a good gasket where the two bowls of a coffee maker are fitted together?

CHAPTER 8

Waffle Irons and Sandwich Grills

So many sandwich grills have been manufactured with interchangeable waffle grids that in order to avoid unnecessary repetition in this discussion we shall treat sandwich grills and waffle irons as one appliance. Of course, thousands of waffle irons have been produced without this optional toasting accessory, but excepting the grids there is little or no difference in the general structure of these two appliances.

COMPONENTS

8-1. Electrical Parts. These comprise two heating elements—usually connected in series—one for the upper grid and one for the lower, and the cord set. In addition to the foregoing parts, automatic models feature a variable thermostat and, in most makes, a pilot lamp to indicate when the desired temperature has been reached.

8-2. Principal Mechanical Parts. The upper-grid-assembly leveling hinge, though it has a round hinge pin fitted into a round hole in one hinge member as in any other hinge, has an elongated hole in the other member so that the upper grid, when it is closed, will automatically adjust itself as the waffle batter rises. In the sandwich toaster, this self-leveling hinge permits the upper grid to rest squarely on the upper side of a sandwich of almost any thickness.   In nearly every sandwich grill the upper-grid handle is so designed that it can be flipped over to serve as a foot to support the upper grid when it is turned 180 degrees, in which position the area of both grids is available for frying.   Other mechanical parts include the heating-unit reflector or baffle, the outer shell, the base, the handles, and the feet which obviously warrant no detailed description.

TESTING

This procedure will serve for both sandwich toasters and waffle irons, automatic and uncontrolled.   When you test nonautomatic models, simply ignore the references to the thermostat.

8-3. A Four-step Test.   After padding the workbench with a clean, dry cloth, make a visual examination of the appliance for possible exterior damage.   Then using the same series tester as that suggested for other appliances, proceed with the electrical test as follows:

1. Turn the control dial to its highest point, and test the cord set as recommended in Art. 2-1 or 2-2, whichever is applicable.   If it is faulty, attach a test cord and continue as follows:

2. The appliance now should be connected to the series tester with a good cord.   If the test lamp is lighted, close the 1,000-watt tester-coil switch; the lamp should dim to about half its normal brilliance.   See Fig. 8-1.   If the test lamp did not dim, a short circuit is indicated in the appliance; if the lamp did not light at all, an open circuit is the fault and you must—in either case—expose enough of the interior to test the parts separately with the prods.   If the appliance responds favorably to this test, continue as follows:

3. With the grill or waffle iron still connected to the series tester and the 1,000-watt switch still closed, attach the ground-detector lead to the appliance and revolve the control dial from one extreme to the other to make certain that the circuit remains closed through all the *on* positions and

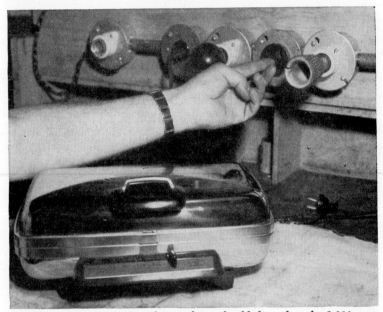

Fig. 8-1.   Testing step 2.   The test lamp should dim when the 1,000-watt tester-coil switch is closed.

that it goes off at the *off* point. See Fig. 8-2. Now, to test the hinge wires, set the control dial at any *on* spot and raise and lower the upper grid repeatedly. Watch not only the series lamp, but also the ground-detector lamp during this entire testing step to ensure that no grounds occur at any point on the control dial or when the upper grid is raised and lowered. Transpose the polarity of the circuit by reversing the attachment plug terminals in the series test receptacle, and repeat this entire step. If the appliance is grounded, you must correct this fault before continuing. If it passes this test, it is ready for the final step which follows.

4. With the ground-detector lead attached, connect the waffle iron or grill to a power outlet equipped with a pilot

Fig. 8-2. Testing step 3. The ground-detector lead can be seen clipped to the right-rear corner of the grill.

lamp, set the control dial at *medium*, and allow the thermostat to cycle two or three times. You can run a temperature test in most cases by laying the thermal junction of the temperature-meter leads in the center of the lower grid. See Fig. 8-3. (Use the same temperature-meter lead assembly for this purpose as that suggested for roasters.) No general temperature tolerances would be of any value here, however, as these vary with different manufacturers. Consult your service manual for the make under test to ascertain the exact temperatures recommended.

Fig. 8-3. Testing step 4. (Operating test.) Note the temperature-meter leads emerging from between the grids just below the ground-detector lead.

SERVICING

Whenever you are called upon to service any of the standard makes of sandwich toasters or waffle irons, bear in mind that to turn out a satisfactory job you must use genuine parts. Infrequently, you may have to repair a nameless grill or waffler to accommodate a good customer, in which case you will be forced to use some type of replacement or fit-all parts, but if the appliance has a name, order the parts from the manufacturer or from his nearest service station.

8-4. Elements. A few manufacturers employ some form of sheathed heating element, others use the common open-coil type stretched tautly through nonflammable bushings or around spools.

At least one manufacturer uses graded elements. When ordering a new element for one of this make it is important therefore to mention the grade number of the old element in addition to the make, model, serial number, and whether

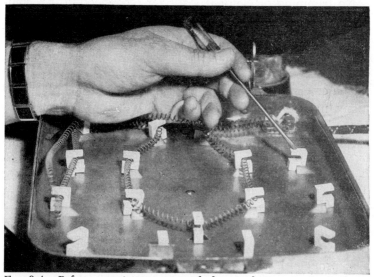

FIG. 8-4. Before renewing an open-coil element, be sure to check the insulating supports. Each must be intact and securely fastened.

an upper or lower element is desired. Following this precaution will ensure equal temperatures in the two grids after element replacement.

Before replacing an open-coil element make sure that every insulating support is in good condition and is securely fastened, for a chipped, broken, loose, or missing support will allow the element to sag and later result in a ground. See Fig. 8-4. Remember, too, when you stretch the new coil to somewhat less than the required length, to stretch it evenly throughout so that no hot spots will be formed. As you thread the new element through the bushings or around the spools, keep a uniform tension on the coil, also to avoid the forming of hot spots and to prevent sagging.

Use the same method of connecting the new element leads as the original unless the manufacturer's service manual offers an optional method for field service.

No trimming of element leads for reconnecting is recommended because with two elements connected in series, any shortening of one or the other will result in unequal heat intensity.

8-5. Hinge Wires.   These asbestos-insulated flexible leads which connect the upper and the lower grid elements are in many models concealed in the hinge, in which case the hinge is entirely enclosed to protect the wires from mechanical injury.   Additional protection for these wires is provided in some makes by the armoring of each insulated conductor with a closed steel spring.   Some makes have been designed with the leads outside the hinge, in which case these wires are nearly always armored.

When replacement is required, be sure to replace *both* wires with precisely the right kind, use extreme care to ensure proper placement and thus avoid pinching, and allow enough length so that the grids will not be hinge-bound. See Fig. 8-5.   And, inasmuch as a broken or kinked spring armor is certain to cause a ground in time, it is also a good idea to replace both the armor and the wires whenever either is damaged.

8-6. Thermostat.   Before concluding from the customer's statement that an adjustment or a replacement of the thermostat is needed, disregard for the moment the hackneyed proverb—"the customer is always right"—and try to find out if the customer is following the operating instructions.   Experience has proved that the customer is not always right with respect to complaints of inaccurate thermostat operation in waffle irons.   This may be explained by saying that waffle irons are not used every day as are most other table appliances and for that reason customers do not get thoroughly used to them as quickly.   Moreover, women are prone to add their personal touch to any recipe—more of this or that or less of something else—but there is a limit to

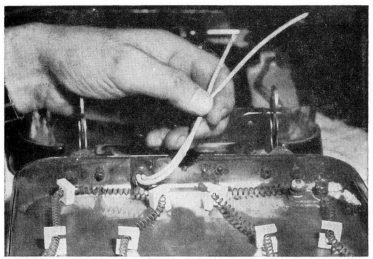

Fig. 8-5. Hinge-wire replacement. Always renew both wires and allow enough length so that the grids will not be hinge-bound.

waffle-iron recipe juggling. Be careful though, in making inquiries that you do not become involved in a dispute. Neither should you take what seems to be the easy way out and replace the thermostat anyhow, for if there is nothing wrong with it you'll get the appliance back for service after the next time it is used.   What, then, is the answer?

If every other part of the waffle iron is in good working order and the grids are properly seasoned, run a temperature test and check your readings with those recommended in the manufacturer's service manual.   If this test discloses that your readings are within reasonable limits, take the thing home and make waffles in it yourself.   Meanwhile, order a few extra instruction booklets from your jobber or manufacturer so that you will have one handy when the appliance is returned to the customer.   Then when she does call for the waffle iron you can explain tactfully that possibly some detail of the operating instructions may have been overlooked, for you not only have tested every function of the appliance with instruments, but also you have made waffles in it.   This may give you the ideal opening to ask: "Would you mind if we skim over the instructions together?"   Then check off point by point every detail that will ensure satisfactory results.   Be sure to use extreme tact as most women are rather touchy about being told how to cook anything.

8-7. Pilot Lamp.   These are in most makes low-voltage bulbs, similar to those used in radios, but you must use the special type supplied by the manufacturer for use in waffle irons and grills because of the high temperature in the pilot-lamp enclosure.   As explained in Art. 6-10, these low-voltage lamps also may be tested with a single flashlight cell. When you do replace a pilot lamp, always check the connections on its resistor to see that they are tight, for a loose connection here will cause repeated lamp burnouts.

8-8. Grids.   Warped grids, of course, must be replaced. Grids which have become severely blackened may be cleaned *on the cooking side only* with a wire brush, after which they must be reconditioned (or reseasoned).   This process is accomplished by heating the grids to a medium temperature and then applying unsalted vegetable oil to both grids with a pastry brush.   Then allow the waffle iron to continue heating for about ten minutes.

8-9. Cord Set and Terminals.   As in all other appliances, the terminal pins and the terminal plug contacts must be clean and bright to ensure a good electrical connection.   If the terminals are burned as a result of a loosely connected cord set and they cannot be satisfactorily cleaned, replace them and the cord set at the same time. Whether built-in or detachable cord sets are used, no patching is warranted except for the replacement of the attachment plug.

8-10. Handles, Feet, and Control Dial. Make certain that these miscellaneous parts are all intact. In sandwich grills and in combination grills and waffle irons remember that the upper grid handle (on makes where it serves this double purpose) must be nicely adjusted so that it will serve as a firm support for the upper grid when it is turned 180 degrees (face upward). Position the control dial so that it indicates *off* at the *off* position.

8-11. Prove the Work. Test the completed job by subjecting it to every step in Art. 8-3. But you do not have to make waffles in every automatic waffle iron you service— the suggestion offered in Art. 8-6 applies only to those difficult cases in which you are reasonably certain that operating instructions are *not* being followed. Another thing, unless your shop is located in a town full of waffle lovers, only about one job in forty will be an automatic waffle iron. So cheer up!

QUESTIONS

1. It has been stressed that you must test automatic heating appliances thoroughly for possible intermittent grounds which can originate in a faulty thermostat as the temperature rises. In addition to this, it is pointed out in *Testing,* step 3, of this chapter that in waffle irons and grills there is another source of possible intermittent grounds. What is it?

2. Under what circumstances would you consider using fit-all parts to repair a grill or waffle iron?

3. Would you attempt to trim and reconnect a heating

element which had burned off an inch or two from a terminal?

4. In stretching a new open-coil heating element just before installing it, should you stretch it to exactly the length of the old one; to a little less than the length of the old one; or somewhat longer than the old one?

5. When renewing hinge wires, what precaution must you take to ensure free movement of the hinge?

6. Explain how you would recondition (or reseason) waffle-iron grids.

CHAPTER 9

Rotisseries

A de luxe model rotisserie features several cooking methods in the one appliance. For example, a whole chicken—or any other piece of meat which will fit into the cooking compartment—may be impaled on the spit where it will be rotated automatically under the broiler heating unit in a manner similar to what you have seen at a roadside barbecue stand. And the top of several models is so designed that it may be utilized for surface cooking or as a warming compartment. Or, if the rotisserie is so equipped, it may be converted into a roaster by inserting an auxiliary bake unit in the bottom of the cooking compartment.

Several manufacturers, however, have produced less elaborate models, some of which feature rotary broiling only, to appeal to purchasers who enjoy this type of cooking but prefer to sacrifice one or more of the de luxe model extras for a lower initial outlay.

COMPONENTS

9-1. The Two Basic Electrical Operating Parts. These comprise (1) the broiler heating unit which, being in the ceiling of the cooking compartment, serves also to heat the pan or the warming compartment on the top side of the appliance, if it is so designed; and (2) the motor which turns the spit. See Figs. 9-1 and 9-2.

9-2. Control and Signaling Devices. Which and how many depend upon the make and model. They include a pilot lamp to indicate when the rotisserie is operating, a buzzer to inform the user when the cooking cycle has been completed, a heat control, a spit motor switch, and a timer.

FIG. 9-1. The broiler heating element. Note that the coils are evenly stretched and taut.

A receptacle to which the bake unit may be connected is provided in the models which have this optional accessory. As a safeguard against overloading the rotisserie wiring as well as the house circuit which would occur if the bake and the broiler units were connected simultaneously, the bake-unit receptacle is controlled by a double-throw switch which will energize the broiler unit in one position and the bake unit in the other.

The heat control used in some models is a type of infinite-control switch. This device controls the temperature of the cooking compartment by periodically interrupting the flow of electrical energy to the heating element. The duration of these interruptions may be varied by the user through the control dial. If the dial is set at one-quarter of full heat, the current will flow to the element 15 seconds out of every minute; at one-half heat, 30 seconds out of each minute; at

Fig. 9-2. One type of motor and gear-box assembly. This picture also shows how neatly interior wiring splices can be made with screw-on wire connectors.

full heat, the current will flow uninterrupted. Hence, an infinite number of variations in heat intensity are available between the high and the low extremes.

Oversimplified for the sake of clarity, here is how this type switch operates: A cam within the switch mechanism is rotated at a constant speed by a motor. (In at least one make rotisserie the spit motor is used for this purpose.) Also into the switch is built a set of normally closed contacts which may be shifted toward the cam or away from it by turning the control dial. Now when the dial is set at the highest heat, the contacts will be just out of reach of the cam so that current will flow uninterrupted. But if the dial is turned to, say, a medium heat, the contacts will be thereby moved into a position where the cam, as it rotates, will open the contacts and hold them open for about half a revolution. If the dial is set at one-quarter heat, the cam will open the contacts and hold them open for three-quarters of a revolution, and so on.

Simple two- or three-heat control in uniform steps is accomplished with a common two- or three-heat switch used in conjunction with a two-element broiler unit. In a broiler unit consisting of two elements of equal wattage, up to three heats may be obtained by switching. High heat is delivered when both elements receive their full-line voltage; medium (or one-half) heat when one of the elements receives its full-line voltage; and low (or one-quarter) heat when the two elements are connected in series. This type of switching may be quite familiar to many readers as it was used in all early-model electric ranges and table stoves.

The purpose of the timer is fully understood even by a layman, and inasmuch as this subassembly is more often renewed than repaired in the field, no detailed discussion of its working parts is called for here. A point of interest, however, is that the timer in some models is powered by the spit motor, some of which are controlled by an on-and-off switch. You must remember, therefore, when servicing a rotisserie of this type that, if the spit-motor switch is turned off, neither the spit nor the timer will operate. Other manufacturers employ an independent timer.

9-3. Principal Mechanical Parts. These include the connecting shafts, the couplings, and the gear train through which motion is conveyed from the motor to the spit (and also to the controls in some models) at a suitable speed.

TESTING

This testing procedure differs somewhat from that suggested for other appliances because in most of the de luxe model rotisseries several current-consuming devices are parallel connected. This means, of course, that if the test lamp glows when the appliance is connected to the series tester, it is difficult to tell—without numerous resistance measurements for various makes and models—which of possibly three functions is inoperative, for the remaining one or two will indicate a closed circuit on the test lamp. The object of this testing plan, therefore, is to rule out as quickly as possible short circuits, open circuits, and grounds. Then you can connect the appliance to full line voltage and find out what works and what doesn't.

As explained in previous chapters it is always desirable to ascertain if possible the cause of failure in any appliance before dismantling it. But wiring designs vary widely with different-make rotisseries and with this thought in mind you will no doubt, after some practice, work out for yourself certain testing short cuts to use on makes you most frequently service. For example, on a model equipped with a bake-unit receptacle and its double-throw switch, you can disconnect the broiler unit for a part of the continuity test if desired by throwing the switch to *bake;* this would leave only the motor and the pilot lamp parallel connected. Obviously, it is a convenience to be able to eliminate without unwiring any single device from a parallel-connected group during a continuity test. Therefore study carefully each model that is new to you so that you may modify the testing plan to suit your needs.

9-4. A Five-step Test. After you have made a careful examination of the appliance and its cord set for exterior damage, pad the workbench with a clean cloth and proceed as follows:

1. Set the timer so that the rotisserie will operate, put the
heat control on *high,* connect the cord set to the series tester
for the continuity test through a 25-watt lamp, and connect

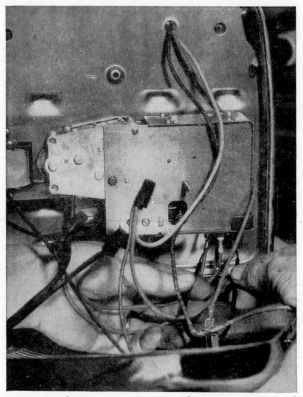

Fig. 9-3. A part of testing step 3. Here the serviceman is touching the
bared ends of a U-shaped piece of wire to the timer terminals to rule out
an open circuit at that point.

the ground-detector lead to some metal part of the rotisserie
body. If the test lamp glows steadily, stress-test the cord
set and, if it responds favorably, omit step 2. If the test
lamp does not light, or if it flickers as a result of a loose connection, continue as follows:

2. Push in the cord and twist it slightly at the ends in an effort to detect a loose connection at the terminals. If this fails to disclose the trouble, expose the cord-connecting terminals and attach a short-circuiting jumper there to enable you to test the cord set separately. If the test lamp

Fig. 9-4. Testing step 4. If the test lamp does not dim when the 1,000-watt tester-coil switch is closed, a short circuit is indicated.

does light now, stress-test the cord set from end to end and, if it is all right, remove the jumper and continue with step 3. If the cord set is faulty, however, remove the jumper and install a test cord before continuing.

3. It is assumed that the rotisserie now has a good cord set. If the test lamp still does not light, make sure first that all the controls are in the operating position and then short-circuit the timer terminals. See Fig. 9-3. If this fails to produce a closed circuit, you must expose enough of the in-

terior to check the wiring and the controls, in which case it is a good idea to look first for a burned-off or disconnected common wire (one that connects one polarity of all current-consuming devices with one line terminal), for it is unlikely that three devices would all develop some integral fault at the same time. If the test lamp does light, continue with the next step.

FIG. 9-5. Testing step 5. Be ready to withdraw the plug from the power outlet immediately to prevent further damage to the motor if it does not revolve when energized.

4. With the rotisserie still connected to the series tester and the ground-detector lead attached, close the 1,000-watt tester-coil switch momentarily. See Fig. 9-4. The test lamp should dim; if it does not, a short circuit is indicated and you must locate the trouble and correct it before proceeding further. If the test lamp did dim when you closed the 1,000-watt tester-coil switch, transpose the polarity of

the circuit by reversing the attachment plug blades in the series test receptacle and repeat the foregoing test. Bear in mind, too, that the ground-indicating lamp should stay off throughout this test. If the rotisserie responds favorably to this step, continue as follows:

5. Leave the ground-indicating test lead attached and connect the rotisserie's cord set to a power outlet equipped with a pilot lamp. See Fig. 9-5. Note quickly whether or not the motor operates; if it does not, disconnect the cord set immediately to avoid further damage and check the motor and its gear train for free movement. Expose enough of the mechanism so that you can isolate the fault to one part or the other and, if you cannot correct the trouble easily at this point, disconnect the motor from the circuit so that you can test the remainder of the electrical parts. If the motor does operate, test the other functions of the rotisserie through their respective controls. Don't forget to glance occasionally toward the ground-indicating lamp to see that it does not light during any stage of operation.

SERVICING

In order to avoid the time-wasting business of tracing interior wiring circuits in the rotisserie, have convenient a wiring diagram for the model in hand before you do any unwiring. But if you cannot obtain for certain models such a diagram, draw one yourself when you dismantle one of these models for the first time and identify the sketches with the make and model number and retain them for reference.

9-5. Element. Sheathed heating units are relatively simple to renew and unless the manufacturer recommends a revised procedure for replacement, merely observe how the original unit was installed and follow the same method.

Open-coil elements, however, require more care in handling and installation.   First of all, make sure that the insulating supports for the element are intact and are securely fastened.   Then stretch the coil evenly throughout its entire length to somewhat less than the required measure so that as you thread it into place you may keep the coil under slight tension.   When properly installed, the coil should be uniformly stretched and taut from end to end.   See Fig. 9-1. If the turns of the coil are more closely gathered in one place than in another, hot spots will occur at these points and uneven heating will result.   It is worth a little extra time, therefore, to work with extreme patience in order to do a good job.   No attempt should be made to patch a heating element.

9-6. Motor and Gears.   Except for minor adjustments you may find it more economical to renew a faulty motor than to repair it.   After ascertaining roughly what parts will be needed—provided the manufacturer will supply individual motor parts—and about how much labor you will expend to install them, compare this estimate with the price of a new motor and install a new one if these two figures are close—even if the cost of a new motor is slightly higher.

When you service the motor and gears assembly, keep in mind that free rotation of all parts is essential and that any linking or connecting shafts must be precisely aligned with their couplings without abnormal end play.   Excessive end play, particularly in a "floating" shaft, will allow it to work away from its coupling socket at one end or the other, with the result that the coupling's indexing member will be "chewed" away gradually until the coupling and/or the shaft end is ruined.

In renewing any of these mechanical parts, therefore, look for the original cause of the trouble and be sure to eliminate that at the same time.   For example, if you come across a damaged coupling or shaft, try to find out why the part failed. You may discover that the shaft and coupling engagement is too shallow, in which case you must realign the other parts to effect a deeper engagement of the indexing members. In the same inquiring manner, look for the cause of gear damage before installing new gears.

9-7. Pilot Lamp. If there is any doubt as to whether the lamp or the socket is at fault, test the bulb separately. Use the test prods in series with a 25-watt lamp to test line-voltage pilot bulbs.

9-8. Bake Unit, Receptacle, and Double-throw Switch. If the rotisserie is equipped with this adjunct the bake unit may be tested separately with the prods, after which you may connect it to the bake-unit receptacle and test the unit for actual heating through the controls. Make sure that the plug fits snugly into the receptacle to ensure a good electrical connection. Also, check the double-throw switch to be certain that its contacts close tightly in both positions.

9-9. Heat Control. Unless the manufacturer's service manual gives specific instructions for adjusting any type of infinite-control switch, no service on this control should be attempted. With this exception, therefore, it is more economical in the long run to replace the control if it is faulty than to repair it.

The simple two- or three-heat manual-control switch used in conjunction with two 115-volt elements presents no problem. If the switch is faulty, renew it. The nominal price of this type switch makes any attempt to repair it a waste of time.

9-10. Timer. Electric, spring-motored, or powered by the spit motor, the timer should be renewed if it is faulty unless the manufacturer's manual gives directions for making adjustments. When you do have to renew a timer, consult first your manual or your jobber to find out whether or not an exchange plan is offered.

9-11. Cord Set, Interior Wiring, and Splices. Make sure that all interior wiring is in good condition and that the splices and other connections are tight. When you remake splices use the same type mechanical connectors as the original. See Fig. 9-2. Renew the cord set if it is faulty with one which equals the original in current-carrying capacity.

Finally, test the completed job thoroughly through all its operating stages with the ground-indicating test lead attached to be sure that every part performs as it should.

QUESTIONS

1. Select from the following statements the one which describes correctly how the infinite-control switch discussed in this chapter regulates the temperature in a rotisserie: (*a*) by means of a rheostat, (*b*) by periodically interrupting the current flow, or (*c*) by the use of a bimetallic thermostat.

2. It is explained in the text that up to three heats may be obtained from a broiler heating unit consisting of two elements of equal wattage by switching. Obviously, high heat is delivered when both elements are connected across the line, and one-half heat when only one of the elements is energized. How are the connections arranged for low (or one-quarter) heat?

3. The "chewing" away of a coupling shaft or one of its couplings usually cannot be regarded as normal wear. What precautions must you take, therefore, to prevent a recurrence of similar trouble?

4. Would you attempt to repair a simple three-heat switch?

5. It has been pointed out herein that the testing plan suggested for rotisseries is intended to enable you to rule

out as quickly as possible three faults, two of which are open circuit and short circuit. What is the other?

6. Assume that you are testing a de luxe model rotisserie and you have established these facts: the timer circuit is closed and the other controls are set to operate, the cord set is sound, and the appliance is connected to a suitable power supply. Yet, every current-consuming component is dead —the line-voltage pilot lamp will not light, the broiler element will not heat, and the motor will not even hum. Which one of the following steps would you take in an effort to locate the fault: (*a*) series-test each component separately, (*b*) break and remake all interior wiring splices, or (*c*) look for a burned-off or disconnected common wire?

CHAPTER 10

How to Set Up Shop

Sometime during your career you may be charged with the responsibility of organizing a small-appliance service enterprise. You may, for example, after acquiring some experience in the business, decide to establish an independent shop; or, if you secure employment with an appliance dealer and it happens that you are his first repairman, you will be faced with at least some of the duties of organizing his service department. So that you will be prepared to seize the most promising opportunity that comes your way, we shall discuss now four fundamentals of organization in this order: (1) inventory, (2) equipment, (3) initial investment, and (4) getting the business.

INVENTORY

In selecting the items for an initial small-appliance parts stock, keep in mind that the demand for certain parts for the older models (which are not interchangeable with those of recent production) gradually diminishes with the obsolescence of the aging appliances. Hence, if you are in doubt as to whether you should stock a particular item, choose the lesser of two evils—wait until a demand has been established.   Naturally, you will want to have on hand most of what you need to render prompt service, but the week or ten-day delay in completing a job now and then occasioned by the back ordering of a seldom-used part is preferred to cluttering your shelves with materials you may never be able to sell.

10-1. Suggested Initial Stock. The classified stock list which follows this paragraph is intended to aid you in selecting the various items for an initial parts inventory.   This modest stock can be built up gradually to suit your specific needs, for after operating about six months you will know better what other items are in demand.   As nearly as possible the parts have been listed in the order most frequently called for so that if you wish to reduce the initial outlay and still be assured you included the fast movers, simply strike out what you do not want from the end of any group.

Irons: Cord sets, handles, miscellaneous hardware, terminal-enclosure covers, pilot lamps, control knobs, and thermostats.

Toasters: Cord sets, plastic parts (such as bases, knobs, handles, etc.), miscellaneous hardware, switches and/or switch parts, elements, carriage-latching parts, and timer or timer components.

Mixers: Whippers, bowls, condensers, miscellaneous hardware, carbon brushes and springs, resistors, governor parts, and gears.

Other Small Appliances: For coffee makers: glass bowls, gaskets, filters, and cord sets.   Percolators: fuses, baskets, pumps, and cord sets.   Roasters, wafflers, and grills: cord sets, pilot lamps, control knobs, terminals, and miscellaneous hardware.   No rotisserie parts should be stocked at the outset.

Miscellaneous Materials: Friction tape, screw-on wire connectors, attachment plugs, assorted eyelets, asbestos string, lubricants, grease solvent, wiping rags, sandpaper, emery cloth, assorted standard hardware, and so on.

10-2. Quantities. For a one-man shop, two or three of each part (for each make) will suffice at the beginning, but keep in mind numerous parts will fit several models of the same make. The miscellaneous materials also should be bought in moderate quantities at first, excepting attachment plugs, wire connectors, and eyelets—these are staple items and they cost much less in lots of fifty or a hundred.

EQUIPMENT

10-3. Shop Furniture. You will need a 5-foot $\times$ 30-inch workbench with a drawer, a stool, a drawer cabinet with approximately 24 subdivided drawers for small parts, and

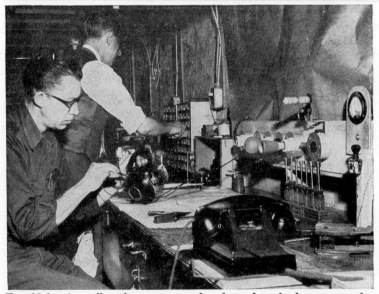

Fɪɢ. 10-1. A small-appliance service shop located in the basement under an appliance dealer's showroom.

about 80 square feet of shelving—roughly 30 square feet of which should be installed beside the workbench for storage of the work in process. See Figs. 10-1 and 10-2.

10-4. Tools. These should include a 3-inch vise, a temperature meter with the electric-iron testing stand and its cable, an oven-testing cable for testing roasters (if you in-

FIG. 10-2. In addition to shelving, drawer cabinets like these make a convenient storage space for repair parts, particularly the smaller items.

tend to use one meter for irons and roasters), an eyelet plier, a tachometer, a hot-water thermometer, and the electrical worker's standard hand tools.

10-5. Series Tester, Ground Detector, and Power Outlet with Pilot Lamp. It is possible that something similar to this equipment, which is described in Chap. 1, can be purchased fully assembled, but you can easily build it yourself using standard electrical supplies for a great deal less.

10-6. Service Literature. Order service manuals, parts catalogues, and parts price lists for every appliance you intend to service.

10-7. Service Counter. The design of this item will depend upon the taste of the individual. For practical purposes, however, the basic requirement is a short counter with two or three shelves underneath to serve as storage

Fig. 10-3. Some shelving behind the service desk for mixer bowls and the like will save steps if the main parts stock is kept on another floor.

space for finished work awaiting call. If the shop is not close by, some shelving behind the counter for mixer and coffee-maker bowls and the like will save steps. See Fig. 10-3.

INITIAL INVESTMENT

Inasmuch as the prices of materials are forever fluctuating, any estimate of an initial investment quoted here in dollars and cents might be out of date before this book could be bound. But there are timeless relative values which we may present that will enable you to estimate rather accurately how long it will take for net profits to offset the original investment.

For example, it may be stated with reasonable certainty that with intelligent buying and careful planning the initial investment for a small-appliance service organization can be offset by net profits in somewhat less than a year—*provided:* (1) all hands are kept busy, (2) selling prices, for both labor and parts, include a fair markup, and (3) operating expenses are in safe proportion to gross income. To illustrate this point, assume that, at prices prevailing at the time you establish a service organization, your initial inventory and equipment would cost $600 to start a one-man shop. Let us suppose also, using the same economic level, that such a shop would gross about $600 a month. From that total revenue, approximately 75 per cent would go for labor and materials, about 15 per cent for operating expenses, leaving a net profit of around 10 per cent which, of course, would offset the original investment in about ten months. But remember, the word used here is *offset,* not *recover;* for in practice one does not usually expect to recover his initial investment in so short a time. Indeed, in almost any new business undertaking, the man who invests both his money and his labor is more likely to utilize most of his profits during the first year or two to expand and improve his facilities in order to satisfy the gradually growing demand for his product or service.

GETTING THE SERVICE BUSINESS

An inexpensive but effective plan to promote a new service organization is absolutely necessary. There are possibly as many ideas on this point as there are businessmen, but five kinds of advertising will get you off to a good start, four of which will keep the customers coming to your shop.

10-8. In the Store. Identify with a small, neat sign the service counter and display some service items thereon.

10-9. The Window. Two or three linear feet of space is all that is needed in which to place an easel-type panel with several repair items attractively arranged and attached thereto; the items could include electric-iron handles, cord sets, control levers, mixer whippers, and so on. Larger parts could be placed beside, and in front of, the panel.

10-10. Direct Mail. Just once, at the outset, send a postal card announcement to the most comprehensive mailing list you can obtain. Have the printer punch a hole in one end of the card—some persons will be more likely to keep the card longer if they can hang it up.

10-11. Telephone Directory. Do not forget to arrange for a listing in the classified section under the appropriate heading. Study the rates carefully, however, before you contract for display space in those yellow pages lest you strain your advertising budget, particularly if you are starting with a one- or a two-man shop.

10-12. Newspaper. Run several lines of classified advertising every day in the service column. The potential income from a relatively small service operation will not warrant display advertising except, of course, where rates are extremely low—as in rural or small community papers. Something every day, no matter how small, pays off better than an occasional splurge.

In writing the advertisement, plan the wording carefully and avoid such terms as *traffic appliances, housewares,* and *table appliances,* for these are trade expressions and they are not yet fully understood by the general public. It is more advisable to head the advertisement with the specific kinds of appliances in the order in which they are most widely used. Even if you list only the first three, such as irons, toasters, and mixers, most readers will get the impression that you do service all the others. See Fig. 10-4.

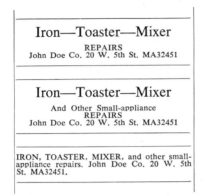

Fig. 10-4. Time-tested classified newspaper advertisements. If your newspaper offers more than one style of type and permits centering the short lines in its classified section, you might like to try either the top or the center advertisement. If such layouts are not permitted, you must use one something like the bottom sample.

Getting the business is as important to you as any of the other three parts of this chapter, for obviously no profit-making enterprise can survive without customers. But in order to hold on to those customers once you get them, it is equally essential that you understand the basic principles of management and ethical business practices peculiar to a small-appliances service organization. Such matters are discussed in the concluding chapter which follows.

QUESTIONS

1. Name the four fundamentals of organizing a small-appliance service operation which were discussed in this chapter.

2. In selecting the items for an initial parts inventory, suppose you must decide whether you should stock a ther-

mostat for an iron which has been out of production for ten years and the parts catalogue tells you that the thermostat in question will fit no other model. Which of the following would be your decision: (*a*) get just one thermostat of that kind with the thought that it would be used sometime, or (*b*) get none until a demand had been established?

3. It is stated in the text that with intelligent planning and wise management, the chances are good that one's original investment in a small-appliance service operation which is kept busy may be offset by net profits in about a year. Does this necessarily mean that the owner should attempt to recover his investment in cash during the first year? Give the reason for your answer.

4. Which of the following plans of regular newspaper advertising for service business would be most effective in the long run: (*a*) one rather large display advertisement appearing monthly, costing about $24, (*b*) a relatively smaller display advertisement appearing weekly, costing $6, or (*c*) a five-line classified advertisement every day, costing $30 a month?

CHAPTER 11

How to Make It Pay

A sound business policy for your service organization is second only to skilled workmanship. This does not mean that you must compile an unwieldy rule book, but to be assured of smooth operation, growing customer good will, prospects (if you sell appliances), and profits, you should have an outline of business procedure to guide your activities. Perhaps you will decide to follow the suggestions presented here either as they are or with some modifications to suit your particular needs. Nevertheless, remember that each subtitle which follows is a point to be settled one way or another, sooner or later. If you take a definite stand on each at the outset, you will be spared innumerable awkward situations.

SCOPE OF OPERATIONS

11-1. How Many Makes? On this point there are two schools of thought: (1) you may want to service all brands for which you can obtain genuine parts at a discount, or (2) if you sell appliances, you may want to confine your service operations to only the brands you sell. Obviously, the first plan requires a somewhat larger parts inventory, but offers in return a larger field of sales prospects; the second, a smaller parts inventory but also a smaller sales prospect potential. All things considered, it is usually more profitable in the long run to service as many makes as you can get genuine parts for at a discount.

11-2. Restricted-service Franchise. But what about the several manufacturers—all respected names in the industry —who will not supply service literature for their products nor grant trade discounts on parts to any but their authorized servicing agents? In the first place, not many of these appliances will be brought to you for service, for most of them will be taken to an authorized service station as suggested in the user's instruction booklet; and, in the second place, what few do come your way should be referred tactfully to the nearest authorized servicing agent. This does not necessarily mean the loss of a prospect even in such isolated cases. Indeed, most persons will appreciate your directing them to where they can obtain the best service available and some will be so impressed with your attitude to service only what you can service well that they may return later to make a substantial purchase.

PRICES AND TERMS

11-3. Parts Pricing. You will no doubt prefer to use the retail price lists of each manufacturer in order to avoid censure in the event that anyone should compare prices— even though the virtually typical 25 per cent off list prices is a rather narrow margin to work on. Some manufacturers with whom you deal may offer somewhat larger parts discounts, but in any case, you must plan your ordering carefully, avoiding small orders whenever possible so that the transit charges will not tend to obliterate the discount.

Occasionally, however, you cannot help ordering a single two- or three-dollar part for one customer because at the time you will have no immediate need for other items from that same source of supply. In such instances you may justifiably add to that customer's service fees the postage as well as any other special handling charges.

If you deal in parts for some of the makes which have no suggested list prices (there are several), the markup is entirely up to you—but it should not be less than 50 per cent.

Miscellaneous standard electrical supplies—such as attachment plugs, screw-on wire connectors, eyelets, fuses, and so forth—which cost but a few cents each, and are usually bought in hundred lots, should be marked up 100 per cent.

11-4. The Service Charge. For an appliance repair job the service charge must cover a great deal more than the labor expended, although this fee is usually computed from the serviceman's working time. To aid you in your effort to arrive at a time charge that will be fair to your customers and reasonably profitable to you, these "hidden" costs have been classified below into three groups. Mull over each a moment or so before getting down to the actual business of setting up a rate:

1. In addition to the overhead chargeable to the service department, an allowance should be included in the time-charge markup to cover the cost of miscellaneous supplies —which never appear separately on the customer's invoice— such as lubricants, cleaning fluid, sandpaper, tape, and asbestos string; under this classification we may also include perishable tools, such as files, drills, hacksaw blades, grinding wheels, and so on.

2. Some lost time is unavoidable, for you must occasionally talk with customers, prepare and quote a few estimates every day (some of which will be rejected), you must telephone a jobber now and then to inquire about a delayed order, and, even if you have a stenographer to typewrite parts

purchase orders, you will have to gather the information for them. Moreover, when parts shipments arrive, you will have to unpack, check, and identify the parts, then allot the items ordered for specific jobs and revive these inactive work orders so that the jobs which have been awaiting parts will be included in the next day's work, and, finally, you must put the remainder of the parts order in the proper stock bins.

Fig. 11-1. You will spend most of your time repairing appliances even in a one-man shop—but no matter how many employees there are, about 20 per cent of a service organization's labor will be used on nonproductive jobs, like ordering parts, quoting prices, tracing delayed orders, and so on. In a larger shop, many of these secondary tasks are handled by a clerical worker.

These necessary though not directly productive duties make it all but impossible for you to collect for more than about 80 per cent of your labor every day—and this proportion varies little with the number of service department employees. See Fig. 11-1. For example, if you are the only man, about 20 per cent of your time will be necessarily nonproductive; if you have three including yourself, two could be fully productive but you would be a semiproductive supervisor; if your organization grows to the extent that you will require four or five men, one will be a nonproductive supervisor.

3. A reasonable allowance must be made for human error, for even the most conscientious and thoroughly skilled mechanic is not infallible. Of the three groups of indirect costs, however, this one is indeed the least—even trivial—but this allowance must be considered along with the rest. In this category will fall not only the reservicing of a repaired appliance under the terms of the service warranty, but also the one-in-a-hundred job which must be reworked before it leaves the bench because of a testing or an assembly error. This does not mean that every rework job is necessitated by a serviceman's mistake, for sometimes you will unintentionally install a faulty new part—one which has suffered concealed damage in transit. You may decide later, when you have had time to study average time charges, to establish flat rates for most of your service operations, but until you do it will pay you in the long run to grant the servicemen under your supervision the privilege of adjusting service charges to a reasonable amount when there is an overrun of labor.

Taking all the foregoing indirect costs into consideration, a suitable retail time charge for service operations may be arrived at by marking up the direct cost of labor from 100 to 150 per cent. If this wide latitude of the suggested markup surprises you, bear in mind that even with equal skill and efficiency the fixed operating or overhead costs will vary greatly with different shops.

The computing of the hourly service charge, however, is the first of two steps in preparing your rate schedule.

For the final step, you should establish a base price for charges up to and including the first half hour which would be somewhat higher for this initial period than for subsequent time charges for the same transaction. In other words, when you have fixed the retail hourly rate, increase the first half-hour charge by approximately 33 per cent additional to arrive at this base price. Remember that handling costs will snatch a bigger bite from your markup as the selling price of a service transaction goes down.

Here is an example: Assume—whether or not you have employees—that you would have to pay $1.50 an hour for labor and, after studying your fixed overhead, you decide to use the minimum markup of 100 per cent. This, of course, would make your retail hourly rate $3.00. Now if you use a half-hour ($1.50) as a minimum time charge, plus 33 per cent ($.50) for the first half hour as suggested above, your rate schedule would read like this: $2.00 for the first half hour or fraction thereof, and $.75 for each quarter hour thereafter.

11-5. Terms. Almost every customer—even those with preferred credit who buy everything else on open account —will expect to pay the service charges when they pick up a repaired appliance. Hence, it is no trouble to maintain a strict C. O. D. policy. Everyone, however, knows his own customers best and you may wish to make an exception once in a while, but a uniform C. O. D. policy does help to hold down costs.

GUARANTEES

11-6. Servicing In-warranty Appliances. Generally, small appliances sold by you and returned to you for servicing within the warranty period should be sent to your nearest authorized service station for adjustment unless you have been appointed an authorized servicing agent for the make in question. There are exceptions, however, as in the case of some minor exterior fault which involves merely the replacement of a control lever, terminal-enclosure cap, or the like. Most manufacturers will not object to your rendering some of these minor exterior services and nearly all will either exchange the part on its return or credit your account for its net price. Needless to say, if you do get permission to handle such minor in-warranty jobs in your own shop, not only will your customers enjoy quicker service in such instances, but also you will be money ahead, for postage and packing would surely exceed the cost of labor for such trivialities. But without the authorized service franchise do not under any circumstances dismantle an in-warranty small appliance, as dismantling without authority constitutes tampering and in such cases the manufacturer is privileged to void the guarantee. When you are in doubt, therefore, as to how far you may go in any specific case of this sort, be sure to contact your jobber first.

11-7. Repaired-appliance Warranty. There are differences of opinion as to how long one should guarantee a repair job—some favor one month, others three, still others one year. Ordinarily, any defective parts or faulty workmanship in a repaired appliance will show up within three months, but to say that you will stand back of the work for a year gives your customers a unique sense of confidence in your ability to turn out a good job. Furthermore, customers' questions relating to the duration of the guarantee are eliminated because your repaired-appliance warranty matches that of a new appliance.

A repaired-appliance warranty, however, is not over-all protection against recurring trouble. Rather, you agree to replace free of charge only the parts which you renewed if any of these prove to be defective within a year (or whatever period you choose) from date of installation. If any other parts fail within the guarantee period, you agree to replace these for the price of the parts only—that is, without a service charge.

Lest by now you be plagued with visions of profits trickling down the drain to pay for reservicing repaired appliances, bear in mind that if you use the equipment and processes described in this book, the need for reservicing will be extremely rare and even in these instances the correction will seldom amount to anything more than a minor adjustment.

RECORDS AND FORMS

11-8. Records. Eventually, you may employ either a full- or a part-time stenographer-bookkeeper. Meanwhile, you must keep accurate records to use as a source of authoritative information in preparing tax reports. If you are not qualified to keep such records yourself, you should engage at least a part-time (nonresident) bookkeeper at the outset.

General correspondence may be stored in standard letter files with the exception of unfilled purchase-order copies and perhaps an extra carbon copy of parts purchase-order follow-up letters; these extra letter copies you will want to attach to their respective purchase-order copies so that you can tell at a glance what effort has been expended to expedite delivery of parts. Even this correspondence, when closed, may be stored in the letter files, but job records should be kept in a separate cabinet.

11-9. The Repair Tag. This is the first printed form to consider and these may be purchased as a stock item with your imprint added or, of course, be made to order by your local printer. See Fig. 11-2. In the stock form there are many styles available, but basically this tag need only be about 3×9 inches overall, with a 3×5-inch center section for the entire job record, a 2×3-inch claim check perforated at the bottom, with another stub about the same size at the top which should be punched for the tag wire. All three parts should bear the tag serial number.

If you decide to have your tags made to order, you may find the following suggestions helpful. The 3×5-inch middle portion of the tag should have spaces designated for this sort of information: date received, customer's full name and address, telephone number, date promised, purchase date (for in-warranty appliances), description of the ap-

Fig. 11-2. Most important single form is the repair tag. This one, re-printed with the permission of Automotive Systems & Forms Company, Inc., 27 Thames Street, New York 6, N.Y., is typical of the three-part tag in general use. On the back: the center portion has spaces for itemizing the materials used; the claim check bears the service organization's name.

pliance (make, model, and serial number), what, if any, parts are missing, as well as what extra parts were received which are not usually considered as belonging to the ap-pliance, the customer's complaint, the completion date, the serviceman's initials, completion notice date, and the de-livery date. On the reverse side of this portion of the tag should be spaces for a list of parts installed, with quantity and part number columns on the left, pricing columns on the right, and a few lines on which to write the service per-formed. Then, along the bottom edge spaces should be provided for the estimate, date quoted, date approved, and the date parts were back ordered.

The punched upper portion of the tag remains on the appliance at all times while it is in your care, and it is important that your imprint appear on this stub, for it will provide positive identification when an occasional job is to be farmed out.

The claim check should bear your imprint, the tag number, possibly a statement of your responsibility regarding unclaimed repairs, and, if you wish, a space for the kind of appliance, but the customer's name should not be written on this part.

Though larger shops may require multiple copies of the repair tag and/or work order, the simple three-part tag suggested here has proved entirely satisfactory for the smaller service organization. And, as you have already noted by now, a common 3×5-inch alphabetical-card file cabinet is all you need for storage of completed job records.

11-10. Purchase-order Forms. Though not absolutely necessary for a small shop, purchase-order forms do save time. Any printer can suggest a number of designs from which you may choose the one best suited to your needs.

When you issue an order for parts, write in (only on the copy for your files) the name of the customer beside any part or group of parts which have been ordered for a specific job. This makes allocation of the parts quite simple on receipt of the order. It will then be understood that any items not so designated have been ordered to replenish your stock.

11-11. Inventory. For a large parts house, a perpetual inventory system is ideal and it serves as an excellent guide to demand, but it can be a nightmare in a small service organization. Unless your business is large enough to support an inventory clerk, therefore, it is more advisable to have your bookkeeper carry an inventory account for the service department which can be reconciled once or twice a year by taking a physical inventory.

Between physical inventories, debits to this account will be taken from repair-parts invoices; credits, from your sales-slip copies on which you will need to show parts and labor separately so that your bookkeeper can cost the parts of each transaction. Miscellaneous supplies which do not appear on the sales slip can be estimated at the close of accounting periods when no physical inventory is taken. Thus, your bookkeeper will be able to give you a rather accurate profit and loss statement at any interval you desire.

11-12. Repair-parts Identification. Every repair part which comes to you unlabeled should be identified immediately after it has been unpacked. This identification consists of four parts: the part name, its number, the brand name, and the kind of appliance for which the part is intended. Tiny items—such as special screws, pins, keys, washers, and so forth—can be put in small-coin envelopes on which the identification may be written. Obviously, a rather large number of these envelopes can be stored economically in an undivided parts cabinet drawer. Or, if you prefer, these very small parts may be kept loose in parts cabinet drawers with honeycomb dividers (about 2 inches square), but compartment labels are somewhat troublesome to make and to attach in these very small cells. Most of the medium-sized parts may be stored unwrapped (but do not remove protective packaging from toaster elements and the like) in drawers with multiple dividers where the contents of each section can be identified with a compartment label. Unless the larger parts have been individually boxed and labeled by the manufacturer, these should be tagged; or, if they are to be stored one kind to a drawer or to a drawer section, the drawer label would suffice. Do not, however, write any prices on the tags, envelopes, or labels, for when you receive a revised price list from a manufacturer it will be much easier to insert the new list or supplement into your price book than to correct prices on perhaps a hundred or more labels.

Furthermore, such a labeling system makes stocktaking a snap. Even an unskilled person can take the inventory in the usual way in the parts storeroom—listing quantities, part numbers, and part names, all grouped under their proper brand-name heading—after which the individual items can be priced, totaled, and discounted at a desk by the same person.

11-13. Parts Price Lists. In order to avoid confusion, it is a good idea to get all service department price lists into one indexed ring binder. Index main sections by appliances, subsections by brand names, and provide at least one indexed section for miscellaneous standard electrical supplies and related hardware which are not identified with any appliance manufacturer. Such a comprehensive price book not only will be an invaluable aid to your bookkeeper for checking invoices and costing parts, but also it will enable sales and/or clerical personnel to complete many a parts sale without your help.

Keep in mind, too, that this "master price list" is the key to all parts supersedures and for this reason the price book should be kept up to date at all times—even though you may be forced from pressure of productive work to defer the insertion of new illustrated sheets into your parts catalogues.

BEST FOOT FORWARD

Ordinary good manners and a refined personality are taken for granted here, but experience has proved that many persons do not at first fully realize the need for a special kind of business courtesy when dealing with service customers.

So that you do not overlook any of the seemingly obvious details, the suggestions which follow are intended to highlight the main points of good service business behavior. Also included under this head are a few of the more common unintentional blunders, some of which border on rudeness.

Let's begin at your service counter where an imaginary customer is waiting, holding a small appliance. Both are ailing, one emotionally, the other physically, and both are to be mended in your establishment. The customer comes first.

11-14. The Initial Contact. That many customers come to an appliance repair shop in a state of distress (some even with a chip on the shoulder) cannot be overemphasized and, further, it is your responsibility to ease that tension as quickly as possible. To this end, get the customer's name immediately after greetings have been exchanged so that in the ensuing conversation you may address her by name. Before taking any further information for the repair tag, however, you should listen with sincere interest to the customer's tale of woe.

And if you have a service counter clerk, it matters not whether it is a man or a woman. A woman can, when it seems fitting, be sincerely sympathetic with another woman who has been inconvenienced by the failure of one of her appliances. If your attendant is a man, the customer will be denied intimate familiarity with her problem, but this deficiency will be offset by the assurance that a *Man* is handling the disabled appliance and is discussing intelligently what can be done to correct the fault.

11-15. Complete Names and Addresses. In addition to the exact address (both mailing and geographical addresses are important in a suburban community whose name differs from that of the rural delivery post office), be sure that you

get the full name of the man of the house. When the cus·
tomer is a woman, the right answer is more likely to come
the first time if the question is put: "What is *the full* name,
please?" rather than: "What is *your first* name?" Make sure,
too, that all names include their appropriate titles. Some
service people may regard this procedure as unnecessarily
detailed, but what extra time is taken (possibly five to ten
minutes a day) will be well spent, for you will thereby double the usefulness of your mailing-list additions. As an example, if you sell new appliances, Mr. Smith may be fully
convinced that the electric shaver described in the circular
you sent him is the best value in town, but he is certain to
buy the shaver elsewhere if you inadvertently addressed the
circular to Mr. Mabel Smith.

11-16. Institution and Business Names. Unless a purchase
order signed by an individual is received before or with the
appliance when one is brought to you for repairs from an
institution or from a business, your service counter clerk
should ask the messenger who brings the appliance for the
name of the person who has authority to act in the organization's behalf.

11-17. Telephone Numbers. Incredible as it may seem,
many persons innocently blunder when asking what should
be one simple question: "What is your telephone number,
please?" Instead, some inexperienced people will preface
this question with another: "Have you a telephone?" You
know the reason—first it was World War II shortages that
hindered expansion of telephone facilities, and now the
building boom in some areas seems to be one jump ahead of
new telephone construction and hence a number of deserv-
ing people in some of these new communities even now
must wait a short while for a telephone. But can you
imagine an eminent professional man being asked *if* he has
a telephone!

11-18. Punctuality Pays. Almost every customer will want to know when her repair job will be completed. And though prompt service is a selling point, a reasonable time must be allowed for processing the work so that every job can be finished in good time. Usually, the three-day method of scheduling (receive it today, repair it tomorrow, issue completion notices the day after) is acceptable to most customers and will allow you to plan your work systematically. When a delay is unavoidable, however, the customer should be informed well in advance of the originally promised completion date.

11-19. Lost Claim Checks. When a customer calls for a repaired appliance and says that she has misplaced or forgotten her claim check, the traditional laundryman's quip, "no checkee, no shirtee," need not be the rule for your service organization. For positive identification—if the person is not remembered, ask for the name and address and a description of the appliance, then compare this information with the job record and, if in agreement, it may be delivered without fear of giving the appliance to the wrong person. But inasmuch as a receipt was given to the customer when the appliance was accepted for repairs, a receipt should also be taken when the appliance is returned. Your attendant should ask the customer in such cases, therefore, to sign your sales slip covering the transaction on the *received by* line.

11-20. Adverse Opinions. Almost every kind of mechanic is inclined to express his opinions occasionally regarding the quality of the products on which he works. We all know that such appraisals are stimulated not only by their knowledge of the inner workings of certain appliances and machines, but also by the questions put to these men by friends and relatives seeking "inside information" prior to making a purchase. But you must be ready with a courteous and *neutral* answer to such questions, for this sort of information amounts to nothing more than an opinion, having no basis in fact, and hence is of little or no value in any event.

Furthermore, be sure that nothing in your attitude, conversation, or gestures even hints to a customer that an appliance brought to you for service is in any way inferior to any other—no matter what you think about it. Indeed, a thoughtless slip of the tongue in this respect can be taken as a gross insult.

One must be careful, too, *how* he says, "We do not repair this make"—if you do not repair every make. Moreover, you must be ready with a tactful answer to the question "Why?" which is certain to follow the foregoing statement.

And do not become involved in the highly controversial subjects of conversation, such as politics, religion, intimate family matters, interracial relations, and so forth. Experience has proved that service people rarely originate such discussions, but often they are innocently drawn in; for some customers, when reciting their appliance troubles, will suddenly go off on a tangent and start talking about anything and everything else from marital mishaps to politics. Shy away gracefully from such topics.

11-21. The Acid Test. On the rare occasion when a recently repaired appliance is returned to your shop for reservicing, you must exercise the utmost tact and self-control because in some instances you may be the object of a scalding initial outburst such as, "My iron is worse than it was before!" or "What *did* you do to my toaster?" This sort of irate customer is easily disarmed. If you will admit that you might have overlooked some detail and express regret that the customer has been inconvenienced by your oversight, the situation is bettered immediately. If a specific case of this kind calls for more balm, you could offer to do the rework job ahead of its turn—even the same day if possible. Strangely, these infrequent reservicing jobs strengthen the ties between you and your customer, for when she calls for the reworked job and learns that you *did* make good your guarantee and that the transaction was handled as promptly and as courteously as the pay-job, her appraisal of the quality of your service shoots up immeasurably. Often, it seems we are more critically judged by the manner in which we correct our errors than by our everyday actions.

QUESTIONS

1. Why is it inadvisable to order less than three dollars' worth of parts from a jobber or a manufacturer?

2. It has been explained with respect to the service charge that the base rate (first half hour or less, for example) should be somewhat higher than subsequent time charges for the same transaction. Why?

3. If you both sell and service appliances, does it necessarily follow that you may repair any of those sold by you during the warranty period. Explain your answer.

4. Should a repaired-appliance warranty entitle the customer to free service on any and all subsequent failures to the expiration of the warranty?

5. Accurate and orderly business records enable you to study your progress with an eye toward improving your methods whereby your chances for success are greatly increased. For what other reason are well-kept records so essential?

6. If you carry parts for more than one brand of appliances, each repair part should have four kinds of identi-

fication. Obviously, one of these is the part name. What are the other three?

7. Parts price lists should be kept up to date at all times for two reasons, one of which is: so that customers will neither be overcharged nor undercharged. What is the other?

8. When a customer brings an appliance to you for service, which of the following questions should you ask immediately after greetings have been exchanged? (*a*) What's wrong with it? (*b*) Do you want an estimate? (*c*) What is your name, please? (*d*) Is it in guarantee?

9. Is anything wrong with the following fragment of conversation? If so, what? "Have you a phone?" a serviceman asks. "Yes," replies the customer. "What is the number, please?" asks the serviceman.

10. In returning a repair job to a customer who has lost her claim check, how would you protect yourself against the potentiality of a second claim later—that is, in the event that a dishonest person should find the claim check and present it to you in an effort to get an appliance of like kind?

11. Why is it advisable to get the full name of the man of the house (rather than his wife's given name) when recording the information on a repair tag?

12. When you receive an appliance for repair from an individual, it is understood that you should record such information as: the customer's full name, the complete address, the telephone number, the dates received and promised, a complete description of the appliance (make, model, serial number, extra parts and/or parts missing), and a brief statement of the customer's complaint. But when you receive an appliance from an institution or from a business, you should record one more piece of essential information. What is it?

13. Name at least three topics of conversation that you should avoid in talking with your customers.

14. Assuming that the serviceman's statement which follows is true, what—if anything—is amiss about his response? Customer: "This is the second time in three years I've had to have a new thermostat put in my iron." Serviceman: "This make is noted for thermostat failures."

Glossary

aligning reamer A bearing tool which, when properly used, is intended to assure an accurate finished bore as well as exact alignment of the reamed bearing with its mate.

alligator clip A wire terminal used on test cords which affords quick and easy temporary connection; so named because its spring-loaded jaws resemble an alligator's.

Alnico magnet A strong permanent magnet.

attachment plug The plug on the end of a cord set used for connecting to the power supply.

back order To order, as parts, materials, and so on, from a supplier.

baffle (heat) A disc or sheet of nonflammable substance interposed between a heat source and its application to ensure uniform distribution of the heat at the point of use.

bake unit A heating unit used in the bottom of a baking enclosure.

bimetallic blade A strip composed of two dissimilar metals, one of which will expand more than the other at a given temperature. Unequal expansion of the components causes the blade to curl proportionately as the temperature rises.

boss A reinforcing protrusion surrounding an opening.

brick The ceramiclike base into which an open-coil heating element is threaded.

broiler unit A heating unit usually located in the ceiling of an ovenlike enclosure.

calibrate To rectify—as a control which functions, but not at the desired time—temperature, or the like.

cleat receptacle One which may be fastened directly to the surface wired over.

collector ring A disc or collar on a rotating part by which electrical contact is made with a stationary member.

compensator In an electric toaster, a device intended to alter automatically the time cycle to suit any starting temperature.

condenser A device which retains an electric charge.

continuity test One to determine whether a circuit is unbroken.

cord guard A spring or rubber sleeve on an appliance cord which is intended to prevent sharp bending where the cord enters its terminal enclosure.

cord set A fully assembled appliance cord with its appurtenances.

coupling A device by which one part of a machine is united with another.

diagonal plier One which will cut off wire close to a terminal even in tight places.

double-throw switch One which will connect one (or one group) of its poles with either of two (or two groups) of its other poles, but not simultaneously.

drill rod Highly polished carbon steel rod of uniform diameter.

Edison-base receptacle The screw-base lampholder most commonly used in residential lighting fixtures.

escapement A device consisting of a spring-loaded gear restrained by a pawl which, when moved, permits but one tooth to escape at a time.

escutcheon A shieldlike disc or plate sometimes used merely for ornamentation or as a name plate, but more frequently for trimming an opening where a control shaft emerges.

feeler gauge A precision instrument comprising an assortment of metal leaves of graded thicknesses for measuring clearances in thousandths of an inch between electrical or mechanical parts.

fillister-head screw One whose head is cylindrical in shape.

floating shaft One which, having no bearings of its own, is supported only by its driving member at one end and by the driven member at the other.

genuine parts Those supplied by the original manufacturer of a product or his successor.

governor A mechanism which utilizes centrifugal force to maintain automatically the speed of a machine.

governor brushes Those which maintain electrical contact between the stationary part of the governor mechanism and the collector ring of its rotating part.

ground 1. An unwilled passage of current from an ungrounded pole in a supply circuit to the frame of an appliance or a machine which threatens the user with shock on contact. 2. To connect to ground, as to a cold water pipe, ground rod, or the like. 3. To connect to the frame of an appliance or a machine.

heater cord Insulated stranded wire especially manufactured for use on heating appliances.

heater plug A heating appliance terminal plug.

heating element The resistance wire or ribbon which, when energized, converts electrical energy into heat.

heating unit A heating element assembled with all its appurtenances.

helical gear One whose teeth are not at right angles to its tread.

hot wire A special wire, used in short lengths in electrical controls, which expands considerably in proportion to its length when heated slightly. Its peculiar characteristic is used to actuate control members.

increment One small addition, as to a time cycle.

indexing member That part of a mechanical coupling and/or its shaft-end which locks each to the other in a certain radial position so that any movement of one is immediately conveyed to the other.

indirect costs General production costs which cannot be charged to any specific job.

infinite-control switch One which affords unlimited variations in heat intensity between the full-heat position and *off* by periodically interrupting the power supply.

inventory account One kept in a ledger whose balance shows only the monetary value of the stock on hand.

jute or twine fillers The reinforcing strands in an appliance cord.

live test One which subjects an appliance to the same or nearly the same sort of operation as it would get in actual use.

miniature receptacle A small screw-base lampholder; flashlight-bulb size.

Nichrome One kind of heating-element resistance wire or ribbon.

open account A customer's account carried by a vendor on which purchases may be made on credit as often as desired and settled at stated intervals, usually monthly.

overshooting Slight overheating on a thermostat's first automatic cutoff.

parallel connection A manner of connecting a group of devices in which one pole of each is connected to one common wire and the other pole of each is connected to a second common wire. Opposed to series connection.

perpetual inventory system A stock control system in which each item is accounted for on a separate card which is kept up to date at all times.

physical inventory A recording of stock on hand obtained by an actual counting of every item.

pilot lamp A lamp to indicate whether a circuit is energized.

pinion The small gear in a set, either helical or spur.

polarized plug One so designed as to assure matching of its poles with those of the receptacle to which it is connected.

pressure plate That immediately above the heating unit in an iron.

prods Solid wire points, with insulated handles, which are spliced to flexible testing leads.

RC wire Rubber-covered wire, as used in interior wiring.

resistor A device which offers opposition to the passage of current.

rheostat A single variable resistor, or a group of resistors equipped with a selector control.

screw extractor A tool—resembling a left-hand-thread tap, but with coarse threads like a drive screw—which may be tightened counterclockwise into a previously drilled pilot hole in a broken-off screw stump to facilitate its removal.

screw-on wire connector A thimble-shaped nut with a tapering internal thread which may be screwed onto the straight bared ends of two or more wires which have been laid side by side to form a compact, insulated, rat-tail splice.

series connection A manner of connecting a group of devices in which one pole of one device is connected to one pole of another, leaving one pole on each end of the series for connecting to a supply or other circuit.

series tester A device for the preliminary testing of appliances in which a lamp and/or other resistance(s) are interposed in one pole of the supply circuit.

series-type commutator motor One whose field coils are connected in series with its commutator brushes.

sheath The protective jacket on a cable or the like.

shim A thin washer, precisely sized, used to eliminate end motion between the shoulder on a shaft and its bearing boss.

short circuit A bypassing, at any point on a circuit, which would forbid passage of current through the entire loop.

soleplate The bottom part of an iron.

spit A pointed shaft.

spring-motored Driven by a spring, as a wind-up clock.

spur gear One whose teeth are at right angles to its tread.

tachometer An instrument for measuring the speed of a revolving part, as a wheel, shaft, or the like.

tapped field Motor field coils to which several leads have been tapped at various points on the winding during manufacture for connecting to a selector switch to provide speed control by varying the resistance in the field.

testing points See PRODS.

thermocouple As referred to herein, is an instrument comprising two wires of dissimilar metals united at one end (the thermal junction) and connected to a temperature meter at the other. A weak electric current is generated in the wires when heat is applied to the thermal junction and this energy is utilized to actuate the meter. Since the pressure of this current varies proportionately with the temperature at the junction, the meter registers rather accurately the temperature of an appliance under test when the junction is placed properly.

three-heat switch One with four positions, *high, medium, low,* and *off,* used in combination with a group of heating elements to provide three heats by various connecting schemes between the supply circuit and the elements.

tin A trade term, meaning to coat with an extremely thin layer of solder (tin and lead).

transpose polarity To interchange the connections to a pair of poles.

waterglass A syruplike, fireproof cement (sodium silicate).

wedges Balancing wedges are added by the manufacturer when necessary to a finished armature to achieve perfect dynamic balance of the assembly. Insulating wedges are inserted into the core slots by the manufacturer to protect the winding as well as to compress it.

worm and worm gear The worm, a spirallike shaft resembling a coarse screw, usually is the driving member; the worm gear (or wheel), the driven member. Considerable power increase and resultant speed reduction are possible with this one stage of gearing and quiet operation is typical.

Index